THE SMALL GOLDEN KEY

OTHER BOOKS BY THINLEY NORBU

White Sail: Crossing the Waves of Ocean Mind to the Serene Continent of the Triple Gems

Magic Dance: The Display of the Self-Nature of the Five Wisdom Dakinis

A Brief Fantasy History of a Himalayan

Gypsy Gossip

Echoes

TRANSLATIONS BY THINLEY NORBU

Patrul Rinpoche: The Propitious Speech from the Beginning, Middle, and End

Sunlight Speech: Dispelling the Darkness of Doubt

THE SMALL GOLDEN KEY

to the Treasure of the Various Essential Necessities of General and Extraordinary Buddhist Dharma

THINLEY NORBU

Translated by
Lisa Anderson

SHAMBHALA
Boulder
1993

SHAMBHALA PUBLICATIONS, INC.
2129 13th Street
Boulder, Colorado 80302

Shambhala Publications makes every effort to print on acid-free, recycled paper.

Shambhala Publications is distributed worldwide by Penguin Random House, Inc., and its subsidiaries.

LIBRARY OF CONGRESS CATALOGING-IN-PUBLICATION DATA

THINLEY, NORBU.
THE SMALL GOLDEN KEY TO THE TREASURE OF THE VARIOUS ESSENTIAL NECESSITIES OF GENERAL AND EXTRAORDINARY BUDDHIST DHARMA / BY THINLEY NORBU; TRANSLATED BY LISA ANDERSON.
P. CM. TRANSLATION FROM TIBETAN.
ORIGINALLY PUBLISHED IN 1977. INCLUDES INDEX.
ISBN 978-0-87773-856-5 (PBK.)
1. RÑIN-MA-PA (SECT) 2. TANTRIC BUDDHISM. I. TITLE.
BQ766.2.T46 1993 92-56459
294.3'923—DC20 CIP

Lama Padmasambhava La Chag Tshel Lo

HOMAGE TO GURU PADMASAMBHAVA

CONTENTS

PREFACE TO THE SECOND EDITION

ACCORDING TO TRADITIONAL Buddhist doctrine, all positive qualities of phenomena, from small, instantaneous, substance qualities to vast, continuous, intangible qualities, come from Dharma. Many different categories and aspects of Dharma exist in order to benefit all beings who have either dull, intermediate, or keen faculties through their general group phenomena and individual personal phenomena. Any kind of Dharma, whether sūtra or mantrayāna, which originates directly from the Buddha's Dharma revealed by the Buddha's followers, is called śāstra.

The śāstras have many qualities, but all these can be synthesized into two precious qualities. As Yig Ngen said, "The śāstras' main qualities are to redeem or purify the enemy which is the passions and to guide from the lower realms to enlightenment." There are countless different śāstras written by countless different followers of the Buddha. For those like me who cannot write according to these two qualities, it seems unnecessary to write at all, especially when I remember Patrul Rinpoche's speech: "Even though hundreds of sublime and intelligent beings have left countless writings and doctrines behind in this world according to their points of view, still, all beings who have infantile mind create more and more appearances of contradictions from these teachings instead of benefitting from them—so if anyone writes more, the result will be just the same." Because of Patrul Rinpoche's speech, a being such as myself, with neurotic mind, became completely discouraged to write anything.

But many sublime saints have said that even if beings do not pay attention to you, you must still try to express even one word of the name of Buddha Dharma. Although, momentarily, beings may have bad conceptions due to their karma, ultimately there is no question that all beings' root circumstance Buddha nature can blossom into enlightenment from the contributing circumstance of their hearing. So, graced by Buddha in this life, I have had the opportunity to express his speech through previous karma, and also to speak freely according to the wishes of individuals through general American democratic free speech phenomena.

Since I came to the West for medical treatment in 1977, at times when my energy was restored, I have written some books in response to the questions of many different Westerners. These books were written according to the capacities of their minds, whether or not they were a benefit for them.

The Small Golden Key to the Treasure of the Various Essential Necessities of General and Extraordinary Buddhist Dharma, which I wrote in Honolulu, is predominantly very compact. In it, I hastily synthesized the essence of different Dharma ideas according to the three yānas.

Echoes contains what I taught in Boudhanath with many international Dharma yogis and yoginīs, using the traditional method of question and answer to connect ordinary experience with sublime Dharma in a flexible way.

After that, between East and West, I wrote *Gypsy Gossip* because there was so much paranoia between the negative and positive fashions of current spiritual ideas and between the different religious habits of nihilists and spiritualists.

Preface to the Second Edition

Through the circumstance of a good friend's desire to know about how the elements work within beings, I wrote *Magic Dance: The Display of the Self-Nature of the Five Wisdom Dakinis* in New York and Paris, very naturally, without putting in many different traditional category systems or ideas.

Then I wrote *Brief Fantasy History of a Himalayan* in the countryside of New York in the springtime amid swaying weeping willow trees because some of my loving American friends requested me to tell my life history. They helped me through their fanatical, positive hallucination phenomena toward me and my speech which is like brass, but which they saw like pure gold and tried to make as an ornament for the Buddha's teaching.

After that, because everyone likes to create contradiction between nihilist scientific and spiritual ideas in this degenerate age, making conflicts between tangible and intangible qualities, I tried to make complementary connections and harmony by writing *White Sail: Crossing the Waves of Ocean Mind to the Serene Continent of Triple Gems.*

Among these books, my friend Pema Tenzin offered to reprint *The Small Golden Key* due to his noble parents' passing, for purification and the accumulation of merit for all sentient beings, including his late mother and father.

So, through the writing of all these books, with the help of my earnest heart fellows who spent their material and energy with pure intention, may all saṃsāra's merit accumulation and all nirvāṇa's wisdom accumulation be gathered together and, like countless clean rivers flowing from different directions, combine and become the same in one measureless profound omniscient wisdom ocean of Buddha.

Thinley Norbu
1984

PREFACE TO THE FIRST EDITION

I HAVE WRITTEN THIS BOOK FOR all those who are practicing Buddha Dharma. It is not intended to be a detailed, exhaustive account, but a seed or key to the teachings of Buddha. After reading it, you can then go on to clarify your doubts, or follow up your interests, by asking a lama or teacher. Here it is important to choose a teacher who is sincere and learned and who really possesses Wisdom Mind. One who does not have these qualities will only give you narrow-minded and misguided explanations. I hope to return to the West soon to continue and expand on the work I have started this time.

While I may not be a very good writer, if you have faith and trust in the teachings of the Buddha, what I have written may help you to understand the Dharma. Even the Buddha himself, when he was a Bodhisattva, before he reached enlightenment, learned from a hunter. So, if you read this book with an open mind and pure intentions, it may be of benefit to you, just as beautiful flowers can grow in a muddy swamp.

As I have not had time to go through this book thoroughly, there may be words or sentences here that are incorrect. If so, please do not make hasty judgments, but try to understand the real meaning behind the words, and if possible, look up the words in Tibetan books.

Preface to the First Edition

Many people asked me to write this, particularly the Very Venerable Masao Ichishima, who suggested that I write something about the history and teachings of the Nyingmapas for students of his Tibetan Buddhism course at the University of Hawaii in Honolulu.

I am very grateful to all those who have helped and encouraged me, particularly Lisa Anderson for translating and John Driver for proofreading, and I dedicate the fruits of their good intentions and kindness to all sentient beings for their everlasting benefit. May they realize the true meaning of Dharma and perfect their practice.

May I, the writer, those who have helped me, and those who read this book, all realize their Buddha nature and become spontaneously one in the maṇḍala of Kuntuzangpo.

Thinley Norbu
1977

INTRODUCTION

THE NUMBER OF BEINGS WHO wander in saṃsāra is as endless as their perceptions, and these perceptions are as limitless as the number of dharmas, but all these dharmas can be contained in the two categories of worldly dharmas and spiritual Dharmas.

Worldly dharmas are endless, but, as the Buddha taught, they are all contained in the "five aggregates" (Skt. skandha; Tib. Phung.po lnga)[1] or the "twelve born and increasing phenomena" (sKye.mchhed bchu.gnyis).[2] The five aggregates are the aggregates of form, feeling, perception, intention, and consciousness. The twelve born and increasing phenomena are the six senses and the objects of these senses.

Spiritual Dharmas are endless, but they are all contained in the Hīnayāna, Mahāyāna, and Vajrayāna teachings of the Buddha.

---

1. *Phung.po*: aggregates; *lnga*: five.
2. *sKye*: to be born or arise; *mchhed*: increase or spread; *bchu.gnyis*: twelve.

I

A BRIEF ACCOUNT OF THE ORIGINS OF BUDDHISM IN INDIA

A GOOD KALPA, OR GOLDEN age, is a fortunate time in which one thousand buddhas will come into this world.[1] We are now in a good kalpa, in the era of the fourth buddha, the Buddha Śākyamuni. When the Buddha Śākyamuni came into the world, he fulfilled the twelve deeds which all Buddhas perform, thereby revealing himself as a buddha. These twelve deeds are:

Leaving Tuṣita heaven (dGa.ldan) for this world (Skt. Jambudvīpa; Tib. 'Dzam.bu.gling) in the form of an ash-white elephant

Entering into the womb of his mother (Skt. Māyā Devī; Tib. sGyu.phrul Lha.mo)

Taking birth in Lumbinī, and then taking seven steps in each of the four directions

Learning the arts, such as writing, mathematics, archery, etc.

Engaging in sports with other young men and enjoying the company of his consorts

1. A complete history of the thousand buddhas can be found in *mDo.sde bskal.bzang*.

Abandoning the princely life at the age of twenty-nine to become a self-ordained monk

Enduring many hardships for six years by the river Nairañjana

Sitting beneath the bodhi tree in Bodhgayā

Defeating hosts of demons that night

Attaining buddhahood at dawn

Turning the Wheel of Dharma at Sārnāth

Passing into nirvāṇa.[2]

According to the teachings of the sūtras, the Buddha turned the Wheel of Dharma three times.[3] In Sārnāth, the Buddha first turned the Wheel of Dharma, teaching the four truths (bDen.pa bzhi) to the five noble ones (lNga.sde bzang.po).[4] These four truths are: suffering, the cause of suffering, the cessation of suffering, and the path leading to the cessation of suffering. These are the foundation of the Hīnayāna teaching.

Later, at Vulture's Peak in Rajgir, the Buddha taught the "Perfection of Wisdom" (Prajñā Pāramitā; Shes.rab.kyi pa.rol.tu phyin.pa), which is the second turning of the Wheel of Dharma called "characteristiclessness" (mTshan.nyid med.pa) to the general gathering of the Saṅgha, including male and female śrāmaṇeras, bhikṣus, and bhikṣunīs, and to the special gathering of bodhisattvas, such as Mañjuśrī ('Jam.dpal bByangs), Avalokiteśvara (sPyan.ras.gzigs), Vajrapāṇi (Phyag.na rDo.rje) and Maitreya (Byams.pa).

Finally, at a place of supernatural beings unknown to ordi-

2. Some explanations of the twelve deeds are slightly different.

3. There are different views and interpretations of the last two turnings of the Wheel of Dharma according to various doctrines. This outline is too brief to include these differences here.

4. In Sanskrit their names are Kauṇḍinya, Aśvajit, Vāṣpa, Mahānāman, and Bhadrika. In Tibetan their names are Kauṇ.ḍinya, rTa.thul, Rlangs.pa, Ming.chen, and bZang.ldan.

nary beings, the Buddha taught the "Doctrine of Absolute Truth" (Don.dam rnam.par nges.pa) to various disciples such as bodhisattvas, gods, nāgas, yakṣas, rākṣasas, and humans. At these times, the Buddha exhibited many miraculous powers of body, speech, and mind.

The full meaning of the Mahāyāna is contained in the Buddha's last two turnings of the Wheel of Dharma where he taught actual relative truth and absolute truth.

According to the teachings of the tantras, the higher Vajrayāna teachings were first taught by the Buddha at the request of King Indrabodhi of Uḍḍiyāna (O.rgyan). In the Vajrayāna teachings, the Buddha taught disciples of superior faculties, who had accumulated great merit, how to transform impure phenomenal appearance into a pure maṇḍala. In order to teach King Indrabodhi, the Buddha emanated the Guhyasamāja maṇḍala (gSang.ba 'Dus.pa), and then bestowed the empowerment of this maṇḍala upon the king and gave him tantric teachings.

At other times, the Buddha prophesied how he would emanate in the future to continue the tantric teachings. In the *Mahāparinirvāṇa Sūtra* (Mya.ngan las 'das.pa'i mdo), he foretold that he would be reborn in a lake. This prophecy was fulfilled by the "lotus-born," Padmasambhava (Pad.ma 'byung.gnas, "Pema Jungne"), who was born from a lotus in a lake. The coming of Pema Jungne was also foretold in many other sūtra and tantra teachings.

According to the Hīnayāna doctrine, when the Buddha passed away, there were seven foremost disciples with whom he left his teachings.[5] According to the Mahāyāna doctrine, his teaching was transmitted through the bodhisattvas, such as Maitreya, Mañjuśrī, etc., to the "six ornaments and the two excellent

5. In Sanskrit, their names are Kāśyapa, Ānanda, Śāṇavāsika, Upagupta, etc. Their names in Tibetan are Ödsung, Kungawo, Shane Göchen, Nyerbe, Phagpa Dhidhika, Nagpopa, and Legthong.

ones" (rGyan drug mchhog gnyis),[6] the "two wonderful teachers" (rMad byung.gi slob.dpon rnam gnyis)[7] and the "four great teachers" (sLob.dpon chhen.po bzhi).[8] The tantric Vajrayāna teachings were transmitted through Vajrapāṇi and the eighty-four mahāsiddhas.

6. In Sanskrit their names are Nāgārjuna, Āryadeva, Asaṅga, Vasubandhu, Guṇaprabha, Śākyaprabha, Dignāga, and Dharmakīrti. In Tibetan their names are Ludrup, Phagpa Lha, Thogme, Yignyen, Yönten Öd, Shakya Öd, Choglang and Chödrag.

7. In Sanskrit their names are Śāntideva and Candragomin. In Tibetan their names are Zhi.ba Lha and Tsan.dra go.mi.

8. In Sanskrit their names are Mahābrāhamaṇa Saraha, Dharmapāla, Rāhula, and Vīrya. In Tibetan their names are Dramze Chenpo Saraha, Khepa Chenpo Palden Chökyong, Tsunpa Chenpo Drachen Dzin, and Lobpön Chenpo Pawo.

2

THE NYINGMAPA LINEAGES

According to the Nyingmapa school, the oldest school of Tibetan Buddhism, all the Buddhist teachings can be collected into nine yānas, or vehicles. These can be categorized into the "Doctrine of Essential Causal Characteristic" (mTshan.nyid rgyu yi theg.pa), or the "Doctrine of Cause," which contains the three vehicles of the śrāvaka, pratyekabuddha, and bodhisattva; and the "Doctrine of Result" ('Bras.bu'i theg.pa), which includes the outer tantra containing the three vehicles of the kriyā, upa, and yoga and the inner tantra containing the three vehicles of the mahāyoga, anuyoga, and atiyoga.

There are two sections of mahāyoga: *tantra* (rGyud.sde) and *sādhana* (sGrub.sde).[1] Within the sādhana section, there are two

1. Within the tantra section, there are four texts: the "Illusory Net of Vajrasattva" tantra (rDo.rje sems.dpa' sgyu'phrul dra.ba), the "Illusory Net of Vairocana" tantra (rNam.par snang.mdzad sgyu'phrul dra.ba), the "Illusory Net of Devi" tantra (Lha.mo sgyu'phrul dra.ba) and the "Illusory Net of Mañjuśrī" tantra ('Jam.dpal sgyu'phrul dra.ba). Within the "Illusory Net of Vajrasattva," there are eight texts, including that of the "Secret Heart Essence" (gSang.ba'i snying.po).

Within the sādhana section, there are eight texts: "Mañjushrī's Body" ('Jam.dpal sku), "Lotus Speech" (Padma gsung), "Wholly Pure Mind" (Yang.dag thugs), "Amṛta Qualities" (bDud.rtsi yon.tan), "Activity of Phurba" (Phur.pa phrin.las), "Command of Mamo" (Ma.mo rbod gtong), "Offering of Praise to Worldly Emanation Deities" ('Jig.rten mchhod.bstod), and "Powerful Activity of Subjugation" (dMod.pa drag.sngags). The practice

subsections of *kama* (bka'.ma), or Buddha's word, and *terma* (gter.ma), or treasure. There are two sections of anuyoga: *sūtra* (mDo)[2] and *sacred precept* or *authorization* (Lung).[3] There are three sections of atiyoga: the outer category of the *mind section* (Sems.sde), in which all phenomena are established as never beyond mind; the inner category of the *vastness section* (kLong.sde), in which all phenomena are established as never beyond always noble profound space; and the secret category of the *essential instructions section* (Man.ngag gi sde), in which the self-nature of all phenomena is itself directly established.

As is further explained in chapter 5, the special highest Nyingmapa teachings are the three vehicles of inner tantra: *Mahāyoga*, which is predominantly the tantric generative phase (rGyud bskyed.pa ma.ha.yo.ga); *Anuyoga*, which is predominantly the precept completive phase (Lung rdzogs.pa a.nu.yo.ga); and *Atiyoga*, which is predominantly the essential instructions of the Great Perfection (Man.ngag rdzogs.pa chhen.po a.ti.yo.ga), in which the generative and completive stages are inseparable.

In the Nyingmapa school, there are three lineages of the transmission of these tantric teachings:[4] the Lineage of Transmission of the Wisdom Mind of the Buddhas (rGyal.ba

---

of all the buddhas is contained in the sādhana, *bDe.gshegs 'dus.pa*. This sādhana condenses the meaning of all of these eight texts in the sādhana section.

All of these tantras and sādhanas can also be interpreted according to any of the inner yogas, as many sublime saints have explained them, according to different points of view, such as in Longchenpa's "Dispelling the Darkness of the Ten Directions" in the precious section of the Great Perfection.

2. The sūtra of Anuyoga is different from the śrāvaka, pratyekabuddha, and bodhisattva sūtras.

3. According to Anuyoga, there are many texts within the root tantras, including the "All-gathering Teaching of Awareness" (Kun.'dus rig.pa'i mdo) and the "Revealing Tantra Teaching of the Gathering of Wisdom" (bShad.rgyud mdo dgongs.pa 'dus.pa).

4. See chapter 4.

dgongs.pa'i brgyud.pa), the Lineage of Transmission by Signs of Vidyādharas (Rig.'dzin brda.yi brgyud.pa), and the Lineage of Oral Transmission by Superior Individuals (Gang.zag snyan khung.gi brgyud.pa).

1. THE TEACHINGS OF THE LINEAGE OF TRANSMISSION OF THE WISDOM MIND OF THE BUDDHAS

These were transmitted by the Buddhas in different ways according to the three kāyas: dharmakāya, sambhogakāya, and nirmāṇakāya.

In the dharmakāya buddhafield, Great Ogmin (Skt. Akaniṣṭa, Tib. 'Og.min Chhenpo), there are "fulfilled bodhisattvas" ('Bras.bu'i sems.dpa') whose wisdom minds are not different from that of the Buddha. They are emanated from Samantabhadra (Kun.tu.bzang.po) or Vajradhara (rDo.rje 'Chang), who are the same essence, the dharmakāya buddha, and all teachings or knowledge are transmitted directly to their wisdom minds.

In the sambhogakāya buddhafield, according to the Mahāyāna teachings, the tenth-stage bodhisattvas are the disciples of the five jinas, or buddhas of the five families. These buddhas give teachings which appear as light from their lips and tongues.

In the nirmāṇakāya buddhafield, Mañjuśrī, Avalokiteśvara, and Vajrapāṇi are the most important teachers. They are the three emanations of the Buddha who represent his body, speech, and mind, respectively. They give teachings to the gods, nāgas, yakṣas, rākṣasas, and humans.

2. THE TEACHINGS OF THE LINEAGE OF TRANSMISSION BY SIGNS OF THE VIDYĀDHARAS

The Buddha prophesied before he passed away that after twenty-eight years,[5] the essential higher Vajrayāna teaching

5. There are several calculations of the correct number of years, which vary because of differences between historical and religious calculations.

would appear in the eastern direction. First, a good omen or sign was to appear to King Ja (Dza), and then the very great higher Vajrayāna teaching would come. At that time, there were "five holy sages" (dam.pa'i rigs.chan dra.ma lnga), four supernatural and one human, who were in samādhi. The supernatural beings were a god, a yakṣa, a rākṣasa, and a nāga.[6] Twenty-eight years after the Buddha passed away, they arose at the same time from their samādhi meditation and gathered at the meteorite-bearing summit of Mount Malaya in South India. They mourned in a twenty-three-verse lamentation, "Oh, alas! We are in deep darkness. If the lamplight of Buddha has gone out, who is going to dispel this world's blindness?" Then Vajrapāṇi, the custodian of tantric teachings, appeared to them and taught the General Sūtra of the Essence of Wisdom (sPyi.mdo dgongs.pa 'dus.pa) and other texts. The rākṣasa, through his supernatural powers, wrote these tantras with ink made of powdered lapis lazuli on sheets of golden paper. Then he miraculously hid the books in the sky.

3. The Teachings of the Lineage of Oral Transmission by Superior Individuals

The fulfillment of the Buddha's prophecy came twenty-eight years after his passing away, when King Ja had seven wonderful dreams which were good omens. Then, miraculously, volumes of eighteen different tantric treatises and a statue of Vajrapāṇi fell like rain upon the palace of the king. He had great faith in the image and prayed to it. Although he had been unable to read the tantric treatises, after praying, he was able to read and immediately understand the Chapter on Beholding the Face of

6. The god's name was Grags.ldan phyogs.skyong, the yakṣa was sKar.mda' gdong, the rākṣasa was bLo.gros thabs.ldan, the nāga was kLu.rgyal 'jog.po, and the human was Dri.med grags.pa.

Vajrasattva (rDo.rje sems.dpa'i zhal mthong gi le'u). After King Ja practiced the teaching in this treatise, Vajrasattva appeared, and the king requested from him the tantric teachings of all the treatises. Vajrasattva told him that his teacher was Vajrapāṇi and instructed him to pray to Vajrapāṇi for these teachings. Since Vajrasattva and Vajrapāṇi are the same in essence and differ only in aspect, when King Ja prayed to Vajrapāṇi, the "empowerment of the wisdom blessing" was bestowed upon him. Having received this, he fully realized the meaning of all the tantric teachings.

King Ja revealed these teachings to Kukkurāja, and thus the lineage was transmitted. Kukkurāja passed on the teachings to one hundred thousand groups of disciples, and also completely transmitted all the tantric teachings to the great Indrabodhi II,[7] who had ten thousand groups of disciples to whom he in turn taught these teachings. Indrabodhi II transmitted the teachings completely to Siṃharāja, who had one thousand groups of disciples. From Siṃharāja, the teachings were perfectly transmitted to Uparāja, who had five hundred groups of disciples. From Uparāja, the teachings were perfectly transmitted to Goma Devī, who had one hundred groups of disciples. All of those who received the tantric teachings attained the unsurpassed level of enlightenment. From Goma Devī, the teachings were perfectly transmitted to Līlāvajra (sGeg.pa'i rDo.rje), who transmitted them perfectly to Buddhaguhya (Sangs.rgyas Sang.ba), who perfectly transmitted the teachings to Vimalamitra and to Padmasambhava. This is predominantly the lineage of Mahāyoga.

Six conditions unfavorable to the practice of Dharma arose: the power of passions became great, the ability and power to practice Dharma decreased, the human lifespan became increas-

7. Not to be confused with Indrabodhi I.

ingly shorter, the great meaning of the Buddha's speech was lost, the "essential heart teaching" was turned into bad doctrine, and the practice of Dharma became so corrupted that it lost its power as an antidote. The secret teachings of Atiyoga, the "Great Perfection" (Skt. Mahāsandhi, Tib. rDzogs.pa Chhen.po), arose when these six unfavorable conditions occurred.

In the country of Uḍḍiyāna, a son was born to Parharānī, King Aśoka's daughter. He was named the excellent Garab Dorje (Hāsyavajra). Vajrasattva appeared to him, bestowed many empowerments upon him, and taught him many tantric Dzogchen verses. He was invested by Vajrasattva as the master of the special doctrine of Great Perfection. Since he had Vajrasattva's blessing of the Great Perfection, his wisdom mind had the realization of the "meaning of tantra" (Don rgyud).[8] Having this wisdom, he also had the realization of the "words of tantra" (Tshig rgyud), and he bestowed this blessing of speech in writing to benefit those of superior faculties who had accumulated great merit.

These realizations were fully transmitted from Garab Dorje to Mañjuśrīmitra ('Jam.dphal bShes.gnyen) to Śri Siṃha to Jñānasūtra to Vimalamitra. From Vimalamitra, all the teachings and realizations were completely transmitted to Padmasambhava, who took these teachings to Tibet.[9]

The three lineages of transmission given above can also be explained in the following way.

> The lineage of Transmission of the Wisdom Mind of the Buddhas comes from Samantabhadra to Vajrasattva;

8. The term *tantra* here is not restricted to its verbal manifestation in particular treatises.

9. All of the lineages explained above were perfectly transmitted to Padmasambhava, who is the holder of these lineages.

The lineage of Transmission by Signs of the Vidyādharas comes from Garab Dorje[10] to Manjuśrīmitra to Śri Siṃha to Jñānasūtra to Vimalamitra to Padmasambhava;[11]

The lineage of Oral Transmission by Superior Individuals comes from Vimalamitra and Padmasambhava to King Thrisong Detsen (Khri.srong lDe'u.btsan) to Yeshe Tshogyal to Vairocana, and so on to our root vajra master.

Within the terma subsection of the sādhana section of Mahāyoga, there is also the lineage of the Distinct Root and Branch Sections of Sādhanas, which originates with Vajradhara's "Spontaneous Teachings of the Dharmatā's Own Sound." These were collected into scriptures by Rigdzin Dorje Chö, also known as Mithod Pachen Dorje Dragpotsel. Khadroma Lekyi Wangmo hid the texts in the stūpa (mChod.rten) called Chödten Dejed Tsegpa. When the time was auspicious, the eight Vidyādharas (Rig.'dzin) took one sādhana scripture each from this stūpa.[12] The tantra of "Jampal Ku" was taken out by Jampal Shenyen, "Padma Sung" was taken out by Nāgārjuna, "Yangdag Thug" was taken out by Hūmkara, "Dudtsi Yönten" was taken out by Vimalamitra, "Phurba Thrinley" was taken out by Padmasambhava, "Mamo Bödtong" was taken out by Dhanasaṃskṛta, "Jigten Chödtöd" was taken out by Rambuguhya, and "Mödpa Dragngag" was taken out by Shāntigarbha. In addition, the sādhana of "Desheg Dupa" was taken out by Padmasambhava. In this way, the lineage comes from these eight Vidyādharas to present root lamas of this lineage.

---

10. Garab Dorje is an emanation of Vajrasattva; therefore, he has inherent within him all of Vajrasattva's wisdom.

11. Vimalamitra and Padmasambhava both were able to take teachings from Garab Dorje because they had wisdom bodies which transcended time.

12. See footnote 1, paragraph 2, on page 7.

3

ORIGINS OF BUDDHISM IN TIBET

THE RELIGION OF TIBET WAS Bönpo from the time of the first king, Nyathri Tsenpo, throughout the reigns of the following ancient kings: the seven Namgyithri, the two Tökyiteng, the six Bargyuleg, the eight Salade, and the five Oggitsen.

During the reign of Nyathri Tsenpo's descendant, King Lha Thothori Nyentsen, Buddhist Dharma emerged in Tibet. The fifth king after King Lha Thothori Nyentsen was King Songtsen Gampo, who introduced the practices of Dharma customs, primarily the code of moral conduct. The fifth king after King Songtsen Gampo was King Thrisong Detsen, the son of King Thride Tsugten. King Thrisong Detsen built the great monastery of Samye and invited the great abbot Śāntarakṣita (mKhyen.kun byang.chhub.sems.dpa'), Pema Jungne, Vimalamitra, and many other great Indian paṇḍitas to Tibet. He also gathered together many very learned Tibetan translators who were incarnations of buddhas and bodhisattvas. Among them were Vairocana, Kawa Paltseg, Chogrolui Gyaltshen, and many others. The paṇḍitas and translators met together and translated into Tibetan the "Doctrine of Cause," the "Doctrine of Result," and the three special highest Nyingmapa teachings of inner tantra.[1] Śāntarakṣita ordained the first monks in Tibet: Ba

1. See chapters 2 and 5.

Thrizig, Ba Salnang, Pagor Vairocana, Ngenlam Gyalwa Chogyang, Ma Rinchenchog, Khön Lui Wangpo Sungwa, and Lasum Gyalwa Changchub. After them, the number of monks in Tibet increased greatly.

Pema Jungne, Vimalamitra, Vairocana, Śāntarakṣita, and many other great saints and scholars gave many teachings to those of superior faculties and taught them how to perform the sādhanas. Pema Jungne took the twenty-five main mahāsiddhas into the maṇḍalas of the "Eight Sādhana Sections" (sGrub.pa bKa'.brgyad) and the "Speech of the Gathering of the Ocean of Dharma" (bKa'.'dus chhos.kyi rgya.mtsho), and then bestowed the empowerment and the teachings of these maṇḍalas upon them. These twenty-five main mahāsiddhas, and many other mahāsiddhas, fully accomplished the sādhana practices. In order to benefit sentient beings in the future, Pema Jungne, Yeshe Tshogyal, Vairocana, and many other great saints hid holy images and dharmas, amṛta, and many blessed articles in the ordinary places of the earth, lakes and oceans, rocks, trees and the sky, and also in the extraordinary places of the four directions and the center. Thus the Buddha's doctrine rose like the sun and spread and flourished throughout Tibet until the time of the great Dharma king, Thri Ralpachen, who was the third king after King Thrisong Detsen. In this way, the Nyingmapa tradition was founded in Tibet.

In similar ways, the Buddhist Dharma spread to Bhutan, Sikkim, China, Thailand, Cambodia, Korea, Japan, Nepal, Ceylon, and many other countries. The Mahāyāna teachings, the teachings of sūtra and tantra, spread especially in Tibet, Bhutan, and Sikkim.

The "four schools"[2] refers to the four Buddhist traditions

2. The term *four schools of thought* can be understood in two different ways. It sometimes refers to the gathering together of Buddhist teachings into the four categories: Vibhāṣa (Bye.brag.smra.ba), Sūtrānta (mDo.sde.pa), Yogā-

which came to Tibet: Nyingmapa, Kagyudpa, Sakyapa, and Gelugpa. These last three are collectively called Sarmapa, or the New School.

What were the causes and circumstances for the arising of the differences between the Nyingmapa and Sarmapa schools?

The Nyingmapa school[3] transmits the teachings which were translated and spread predominantly during the reigns of the kings Songtsen Gampo, Thrisong Detsen, and Thri Ralpachen, as explained above. The older brother of Thri Ralpachen was the king, Lang Darma, who destroyed the general teachings of Buddhism in Tibet. However, the practices of the kama inner Nyingma tantra were continued by those who practiced secretly in caves and mountains, and as laymen. In this way, the lineage of Nyingma kama remains unbroken from its origin until the present time.

When King Lang Darma destroyed Buddhism, he also expelled many of the nobility from Central Tibet, scattering them throughout West Tibet and other places. Unable to bear the suffering and destruction of the Buddhist Dharma caused by Lang Darma, Lhalung Palgyi Dorje, who had been a monk, assassinated the king with a bow and arrow while performing a dance before him.

At that time, three monks, Mar, Yo, and Tsang, escaped to Kham in East Tibet, where they gave ordination to Lachen Gongpa Rabsal, who in turn ordained ten monks, including Lume. Thus, the teachings of the vinaya were transmitted in an unbroken way in East Tibet. Lhalama Yeshe Öd invited Paṇḍita

cāra (Sems.tsam.pa), and Mādhyamika (dBu.ma.pa). The proponents of these doctrines are called in Sanskrit: Vaibhāṣika, Sautrāntika, Yogācārin, and Mādhyamika, respectively. The first two belong to the Hīnayāna, the last two to the Mahāyāna; together, they compose the Vehicle of Cause. The Vehicle of Result includes all the outer and inner tantras. All Buddhist teachings are contained within the vehicles of cause and result. See chapters 2 and 5.

3. Literally, "Old School."

Dharmapāla to come from India to Tibet, and there he ordained three Pālas. Later, the translator Trophu Lotsawa invited Paṇḍita Śākya Srī to come to Tibet, and there he ordained eleven monks, including Śākya Panchen.

Sarmapa, the "New School," arose in Tibet after King Lang Darma's time, when Lhalama Yeshe Öd and Lhatsun Changchub Öd of the royal lineage gathered together many translators, including the great Lotsawa Rinchen Zangpo, and invited Paṇḍita Atīśa to Tibet to retranslate and teach the Buddhist doctrine again. The following is a brief explanation of the different sects within Sarmapa.

Kadampa.[4] Chennga Rinchen Phel said, "Not one syllable of the Buddha's 'word' [bKa'] is without meaning and can be left out. All of the Buddha's 'precepts' [gDams] must be known and understood." All of the meaning of the Buddha's word of the Tripiṭaka (sDe.snod gsum) is gathered together in Atīśa's advice (gDams), which is called "Lam rim," or "stages on the path" suitable for individuals of excellent, medium, and inferior qualities. Atīśa's teachings were spread by many Kadampas, including Dromtön Gyalwe Jungne, Geshe Potowa, Chenngawa, and Phuchungwa.

Kagyudpa.[5] There are two main Kagyudpa lineages. The Shangpa Kagyud comes from Dorje Chang through the two wisdom ḍākinīs, Niguma and Sukhasiddhī, to the mahāsiddha, Khyungpo Naljor. The other lineage comes from Dorje Chang to Tilopa.[6] This lineage was continued by Tilopa's "Four Special Transmissions" (bKa' babs bzhi'i gdams.pa) through

4. bKa' gdams.pa. *bKa'*: the Buddha's word; *gdams*: precepts; *pa*: those who hold to this lineage.

5. bKa' brgyud.pa. *bKa'*: Dorje Chang's word; *brGyud*: the lineage which originates with Dorje Chang; *pa*: those who hold to this lineage.

6. Within the Kagyudpa lineage transmitted through Tilopa, there are four larger and eight smaller lineages.

Nāropa to Marpa Lotsawa. These four doctrines of Tilopa are as follows:[7]

Illusory-body meditation (sGyu.lus) or transference of consciousness meditation ('Pho.ba),
Dream meditation (rMi.lam),
Luminosity meditation ('Od.gsal), and
Tumo meditation (gTum.mo).

Sakyapa.[8] Drogmi Śākya Yeshe, who received all of the secret teachings of the lineage of the mahāsiddha Berwapa (Virūpa), was one of the teachers of Khön Könchog Gyalpo, a direct descendant of Padmasambhava's disciple, Khön Lui Wangpo. There was an area of whitish land near the mountain Wenpori which Khön Könchog Gyalpo examined carefully. Finding it an auspicious place, he built a monastery there. The lineage takes its name from this land, which is called Sakya in Tibetan. This lineage was transmitted by the five Jetsun Gongmas: Yagthrug Sanggye Pal, Rongtön Sheja Kunrig, Reddawa Shönnu Lodrö, Kunga Zangpo, Kunga Gyaltshen, Goram Sönam Sengge, Panchen Shakya Chogden, and many other learned lamas who had the general knowledge of sūtra and tantra and the special knowledge of the mahāsiddha Berwapa's secret teachings. Their special teaching is the "Path and Fruit of the Precious Secret Mantrayāna" (gSang.sngags Rin.po.chhe'i Lam.'bras).

Shijedpa.[9] Shijedpa was started by the great Indian Mahāsiddha, Phachig Dampa Sanggye, who received teachings from many male and female saints. He went to Tibet where he gave

7. Sometimes the order of the doctrines and their explanation varies slightly, according to different teachers.

8. Sa.skya.pa. *Sa*: land; *skya*: whitish; *pa*: those who hold to this lineage.

9. Zhi byed.pa. *Zhi byed*: to pacify all suffering through the practice of tantra and mantra; *pa*: those who hold to this lineage.

his special teachings called the "Threefold Lamp of the Shijed" (Zhi.byed sGron.ma 'Khor.gsum), which are:

Mahāmudrā (Phyag.rgya chhen.po),
Secret Advice of Seeing the Naked Mind (Rig.pa gCher.mthong.gi Man.ngag), and
Precious Advice of Carrying Realization on the Path (rTogs.pa Lam.khyer.gyi gDams.ngag).

His teachings were practiced in Tibet by Masokam Sum, Goshai Naljor Namshi, twenty-four yoginīs, and many others.

Chöd (gChod). This term means to cut through the "four demons of the ego" (bDud bzhi), which are:

the demon which comes with obstruction, impediments, or form (Thogs.bchas bdud),
the demon without obstruction or form (Thogs.med bdud),
the demon of pleasure or enjoyment (dGa' brod bdud), and
the demon of pride (sNyems.byed bdud).

Chöd was first practiced by Machig Labdrön, a great Tibetan saint. She received the teachings of Chöd from her two lamas, Phachig Dampa Sanggye and Kyotön Sönam Lama. She said: "My Dharma is Mahāmudrā" [Phyag.rgya chhen.po chhos]. This means that the outer meaning of the pāramitā of the sūtras and the inner meaning of the unsurpassed tantras are gathered together and practiced. She taught her son and many other disciples her special teaching of Phungpo Zenkyur.[10] By this practice, the temporary benefit of sentient beings, such as the

10. *Phungpo*: skandhas (here, especially form); *zen*: food; *kyur*: to give away as offering or generosity.

alleviation of suffering from sickness, demons, and poverty, and the ultimate benefit to sentient beings, which is the attainment of buddhahood, are achieved.

Jonangpa.[11] Kunpang Thugye Tsöndru gave sūtra and tantra teachings, including the teachings of the "Vajra Yoga," in the Jomonang area of West Tibet, so this lineage takes its name from that place. Later, the "all-knowing" (Kun.mkhyen) Dolpo Sherab Gyaltshen came to Jomonang and gave teachings on "Other Emptiness Mādhyamika" (gZhan.stong dBu.ma). Chogle Namgyal, Kunga Drölchog Tāranātha, and others also came and spread the general Buddhist teachings and the special teachings, including Cakrasaṃvara (bDe.mchhog), Hevajra (dGyes.pa rDo.rje), Guhyasamāja (gSang.ba 'dus.pa), and Kālacakra (Dus.'khor).

Bodongpa takes its name from Bodong Chogle Namgyal, who received the blessing of Sarasvatī and started his special doctrine. Today, there are not many left of this lineage.

Gelugpa.[12] Jetsun Lozang Dragpa combined the teachings of Atīśa's advice, which was the main Kadampa doctrine, and the tantric teachings of the Sarmapa, or New School of Tibetan Buddhism. He built Drog Riwoche Gaden Nampar Gyalwe Ling Monastery. The Gadenpa lineage takes its name from this monastery. Sometimes, Gelugpas are called the "New Kadampas" (bKa'.gdams gsar.ma.ba). Lozang Dragpa had many disciples, including Khedrubje and Gyaltshab Dharma Rinchen, to whom he gave his essential teachings of "The Stages of the Path of Enlightenment" (Byang.chhub lam.gyi rim.pa) and "The Great Tantric Stages" (sNgags.rim chhen.mo).

11. *Jonang*: an area in West Tibet; *pa*: those who hold to this lineage.
12. dGe.lugs.pa. *dGe*: virtue; *lugs*: system or custom; *pa*: those holding to this lineage.

This is a description of the "eight schools of Tibetan Buddhism" (Bod.kyi bstan.pa'i shing.rta brgyad). These eight schools can all be collected together into the four schools of the Nyingmapa, Kagyudpa, Sakyapa, and Gelugpa.

4

NYINGMAPA KAMA AND TERMA

KAMA (BKA'.MA) ARE THE SPOken teachings which come from Dorje Chang to one's present root guru in an unbroken lineage. The three lineages of kama[1] are the Lineage of Transmission of the Wisdom Mind of the Buddhas, the Lineage of Transmission by Signs of the Vidyādharas, and the Lineage of Oral Transmission by Supreme Individuals.

Terma (gTer.ma) are the precious sacred articles and Dharmas which were hidden until the time was appropriate for them to be revealed. These terma were hidden by Padmasambhava and other tertöns, great saints having special marks or signs, in the ordinary places of the earth, lakes and oceans, rocks, trees, and the sky, and in the extraordinary places of the four directions and the center. At the times when the terma are of most benefit, the tertöns uncover these sacred treasures.

The Three Special Lineages of Terma (Khyad.par gyi brgyud.pa gsum) are:

Prophetic gift (bKa'.babs lung.bstan),

Empowerment by resolve (sMon.lam dbang.bskur) of the Buddha, Padmasambhava, etc., and

1. See chapter 2.

Sealed entrustment to ḍākinīs (mKha'.'gro gtad.rgya) to bestow only on tertöns.

In the past, when the time was right, many tertöns of these lineages have incarnated. These tertöns included the "three supreme tulkus" (mChhog.gi sprul.sku rnam gsum), who were Guru Chöwang, Nyangral Nyima Ödzer, and Rigdzin Gödem; the "five tertön kings" (gTer.ston rgyal.po lnga); the "eleven unerring lingpas" ('Khrul.med gling.pa bchu.gchig); the "one hundred great tertöns" (gTer.chhen brgya); and the "one thousand minor tertöns" (gTer.phran stong.phrag). These tertöns discovered terma "representing the wisdom body of the Buddha" (sKu.rten), such as statues or images; "representing the wisdom speech of the Buddha" (gSung.rten), such as Dharma and special condensed texts in gold and other precious materials; and "representing the wisdom mind of the Buddha" (Thugs.rten), such as dorjes (vajra) which are symbols of wisdom, and phurbas (kīla), which are symbols of activity, and other precious treasures such as amṛta, hidden holy places, and so on.

Terma includes texts, such as the *Heart Sūtra*, which was brought by Nāgārjuna from the nāgas; the tantras, which came from Ugyen Khadroling, a hidden sacred place known only to special beings; and the inventory (dKar.chhag), which paṇḍita Atīśa took from the pillar in the Jokhang. Further information about terma can be found in many sūtra and tantra texts such as "The Brief Sūtra of the Nāga King" (kLu.yi rgyal.po'i sdus.pa'i mdo).

Great lamas, including So Yeshe Wangchug, Zur Sherab Jungne, and Nub Lachen Jangnying, spread the kama teachings of Nyingmapa. Many superior lamas, including the all-knowing Kunkhyen Longchen Rabjam, Minling Terchen, and other learned, saintly lamas, combined the teaching of kama and terma and then spread these teachings.

5

THE DIFFERENCES BETWEEN THE BUDDHA'S HĪNAYĀNA, MAHĀYĀNA, AND VAJRAYĀNA TEACHINGS

THE ESSENCE OF THE HĪNAYĀNA vows, which are the codes of moral discipline, is weariness of saṃsāra. The essence of the Mahāyāna vows is bodhicitta, the aspiration to help all sentient beings attain liberation from the suffering of saṃsāra. The essence of the Vajrayāna vows is the practice of seeing all phenomena as the pure maṇḍala of deities. But whoever enters the Mahāyāna or Vajrayāna path should not think that the Hīnayāna path is not included within the Mahāyāna and Vajrayāna. The Hīnayāna path is automatically contained in the Mahāyāna path, and the Hīnayāna and Mahāyāna paths are automatically contained in the Vajrayāna path.

Pure bodhicitta arises upon seeing the endless suffering of all beings in saṃsāra. Because of this, weariness of saṃsāra is automatically included in bodhicitta. The practice of seeing all phenomena as the pure maṇḍala of deities comes from the knowledge that all impure perception of saṃsāra is no more than the object created by one's own projections, that there is no other saṃsāra than this. By purifying one's projection of phenomena, one ceases to grasp at saṃsāra as being real and thus weariness of saṃsāra is automatically included in this pure perception. The practice of seeing all beings as deities in the maṇḍala automatically includes bodhicitta because one sees all beings as enlightened Buddhas, beyond the suffering of saṃsāra.

Why are there differences between the Buddha's Hīnayāna, Mahāyāna, and Vajrayāna teachings?

Because the Buddha was omniscient, he could teach according to the minds, perceptions, and passions of each individual. Accordingly, the Hīnayāna teaches that the passions must be abandoned; the Mahāyāna teaches that the passions must be changed; and the higher Vajrayāna teaches that the passions must be relied upon.

For example, according to the Hīnayāna, if desire for a woman arises, this desire must be abandoned. The antidote is to meditate on the "nine disgusting things" (Mi sdug.pa dgu), and with the perception of the woman as disgusting, desire vanishes. According to the Mahāyāna, if desire for a woman arises, it must be changed. The antidote is to meditate on her as being an illusion arising from one's own phenomenal projections; when one perceives her in this way, desire vanishes. According to the higher Vajrayāna, if desire for a woman arises, it must be relied upon, and through good practice of the "generative phase" (bsKyed.rim) and "completive phase" (rDzogs.rim) of meditation, one can visualize women as ḍākinī consorts so that all phenomena become the pure maṇḍala of the deities and all ordinary desire vanishes. Thus, in the higher Vajrayāna, it is not necessary to meditate on women either as disgusting or as being an illusion.[1]

1. Of course, these methods also apply to women's perceptions of men.

According to the Hīnayāna code of moral discipline, the passions must be abandoned; they are like a poison which is fatal, so one avoids them. According to the Mahāyāna practice of bodhicitta, one cannot use the passions for one's own benefit, but can use them for the benefit of others; they are like a poison which can be neutralized by its antidote so that it can be taken harmlessly. According to the higher Vajrayāna practice of transforming all phenomena into the maṇḍala of the deities, one can rely upon the passions for one's practice; they are like a poison which is recognized as medicine.

The Wisdom Mind of the Buddha is perfect, so there is no need to doubt any of his teachings. We individuals should not insult the teachings of the Buddha by forming judgments with our narrow, neurotic minds. We should examine carefully the three disciplines of the Hīnayāna, Mahāyāna, and Vajrayāna, and then decide if we wish to accept just one, two, or all three disciplines together. This is the Nyingmapa system. For more explanations and details about this, one can read books by Kunkhyen Longchenpa, Ngari Panchen, Pema Wanggyal, Minling Dochen, Dharma Shrī, Rigdzin Jigme Lingpa and Jamyang Mipham.

The "two egoless states" (bDag.med gnyis) are egolessness of the self (Gang.zag.gi bdag.med) and the egolessness (or insubstantiality) of phenomena (Chhos. kyi bdag.med). It is said that the habit of "individual ego (or self)" (Gang.zag) is continuous.[2] The basic attachment of supposing "I am" is the "holding to the ego (or self)" (Gang.zag.gi bdag). When one realizes that there is no ego, then this is the realization of the state of "egolessness of self." But until this is realized, one clings to the idea of an ego and perpetuates it, thus making the

2. *Gang* means "full": the mind is filled with passions. *Zag* means "fall down": because of passions, sentient beings fall down into saṃsāra.

ego continuous. The inherent aim of the ego is to make itself continuous. For this reason, the ego is said to be inherently continuous. This holding to one's ego or self as real is the "obscuration of the passions" (Nyon.mongs.pa'i sgrib.pa).

Chhos has many meanings, but here it means the phenomena which one regards or holds to as being real. All the phenomena of saṃsāra are created by the "object grasped" (gZung.ba yul), and the "mind which grasps the object" ('Dzin.pa sems). That is, first the mind perceives that there is an object, and then the mind seizes hold of this object. This is "holding to the ego (or substantiality) of phenomena" (Chhos kyi bdag). Holding to phenomena as real is the "obscuration of not knowing" (Shes.bya'i sgrib.pa).

For example, when experiences of bliss, luminosity, and great emptiness arise while meditating, thinking "This is my bliss, my luminosity, my great emptiness" is "holding to ego (or self)." The belief that there is bliss, luminosity, and great emptiness, that they really exist, is "holding to the ego (or substantiality) of phenomena."

There are a number of systems of explaining the "holding to the ego of phenomena," but they can all be condensed into the systems discussed above.

Since the "obscuration of passions" arises from "holding to the ego or self," one must realize the "egolessness of self" to purify this obscuration. Since the "obscuration of not knowing" comes from "holding to the ego of phenomena," one must realize the "egolessness of phenomena" to purify this obscuration.

THE NINE YĀNAS

As explained in chapter 2, all the Nyingmapa teachings are contained in the teachings of the nine yānas: the three vehicles of the "Doctrine of Cause,"[3] which includes śrāvaka, pratyekabuddha, and bodhisattva; and the six vehicles of the "Doctrine of Result,"[4] which includes the three vehicles of outer tantra, Kriyā, Upa, and Yoga; and the three vehicles of inner tantra, Mahāyoga, Anuyoga, and Atiyoga.

These nine yānas can be explained through their different views, practices (including meditation), activities, and results.

THE THREE VEHICLES OF THE DOCTRINE OF CAUSE

1. According to the basic Hīnayāna Śrāvakayāna, the view is the realization of the "egolessness of self." When this is realized, the obscuration of the passions is purified. But because the śrāvakas predominantly hold to the object grasped as being composed of extremely subtle particles, and are absolutely determined that the mind which grasps is composed of instantaneous indivisible particles, they believe that the subtle particles which compose the object and the mind are the root basis of phenomena and the support of karma and its result. This is "holding to the ego (or substantiality) of phenomena." The activity is the practice of morality, observing the vinaya, or the two hundred and fifty monastic vows. The practice of meditation is on the "nine disgusting things," etc., to subdue the mind to attain shine (Skt. śamatha; Tib. Zhi.gnas), or tranquillity meditation; and on the "sixteen impermanences," including the "four truths," to pacify the mind to attain lhagtong (Skt. vipaśyanā; Tib. Lhag.thong), or "sublime-seeing" meditation. The result is the attainment of the state of arhat.

2. According to the basic Pratyekabuddhayāna, the view is the realization of the "egolessness of self," and the half-realiza-

3. The doctrine of cause is so called because in these yānas one's practice uses the cause of buddhahood.

4. The doctrine of result is so called because in these yānas one's practice uses the result of buddhahood.

tion of the "egolessness (or insubstantiality) of phenomena," since they realize that the "object held to has no true nature" (gZung.ba yul rang.bzhin med.pa rtogs), but believe that the instantaneous indivisible particle of the mind is the basis of phenomena and the support of karma and its result. The activity is similar to śrāvaka practice and may be carried on in company with others (Tshogs.na spyod.pa) or in solitude (bSer.ru lta.bu). The practice is meditation on the "twelve interdependent links of causation" (Skt. nidāna; Tib. rTen.hbrel bchu.gnyis) by meditating in reverse on the succession of the twelve "interdependent links" (Lugs.'byung lugs.ldog).

The twelve interdependent links of causation are:

Ignorance (Skt. avidyā; Tib. Ma.rig.pa): ignorance arises through not recognizing, for countless previous lives, the completely pure meaning which is the basic condition of the nature of the mind and the skillful means or ability of the mind;

Perception (Skt. saṃskāra; Tib. 'Du.byed): the result of this ignorance of countless previous lives is rebirth and the body we have in this present life; because of this ignorance we continue to make karma and have the perception of saṃsāra;

Consciousness (Skt. vijñāna; Tib. rNam.par shes.pa): through this perception we fall into saṃsāra and consciousness is formed;

Name and form (Skt. nāma-rūpa; Tib. Ming.gzugs): consciousness then creates the appearance of objects (Tib. Yul) and of various names and forms of these objects;

Six senses (Skt. ṣaḍāyatana; Tib. sKye.mchhed drug): from the distinctions of name and form, the distinctions of the six senses, colors, elements, etc., are made;

Contact (Skt. sparśa; Tib. Reg.pa): from these six senses comes contact when the object, the senses, and consciousness all come together;

Feelings or sensation (Skt. vedanā; Tib. Tshor.ba): through contact with objects, feelings or sensations of bliss, suffering, and indifference arise;

Desire (Skt. tṛṣnā; Tib. Sred.pa): depending on these feelings, desire arises in the mind to grasp the feelings of bliss and happiness and to reject the feelings of suffering and unhappiness;

Grasping (Skt. upādāna; Tib. Len.pa): because of this desire, grasping at the object arises;

Coming into being (samsaric existence) (Skt. bhava; Tib. Srid.pa): continual grasping to objects makes and increases the passions and karma, forms future karma, and causes continual coming into being and samsaric existence;

Rebirth (Skt. jāti; Tib. sKye.ba): from coming into being and samsaric existence comes rebirth in the many various forms within the six realms of beings; and

Old age and death (Skt. jarā-maraṇa; Tib. rGa.shi): from this rebirth comes old age and death.

The result of meditating upon these interdependent links is the attainment of the state of pratyekabuddhahood by oneself in a place where there are no other buddhas.

3. According to the basic bodhisattvayāna, the view is the "two egoless states": "egolessness of self" and "egolessness (or insubstantiality) of phenomena." The activity is the practice of the "six or ten pāramitās" and the "four ways to benefit others" (Tib. bsDu.ba'i dngos.po bzhi). The six or ten pāramitās are generosity (Skt. dāna; Tib. Sbyin.pa), morality (Skt. śīla; Tib. Tshul.khrims), patience (Skt. Kṣanti, Tib. bZod.pa), diligence (Skt. vīrya; Tib. brTson.'grus), meditation (Skt. dhyāna; Tib. bSam.gtan), sherab-wisdom (Skt. prajñā; Tib. Shes.rab), and also skillful means (of mind) (Skt. upāya; Tib. Thabs), power

(Skt. bala; Tib. sTobs), aspiration (Skt. praṇidhāṇa, Tib. sMon.lam), and yeshe-wisdom (Skt. jñāna; Tib. Ye.shes). The four ways to benefit others are giving, using meaningfully pleasing speech, using oneself according to Dharma custom, and inspiring others through the speech of meaningful Dharma practice. The practice is the "thirty-seven practices of a bodhisattva" (Byang.chhub phyogs.kyi chhos sum.chu.so.bdun), which are the first four of the "five paths" (Lam.lnga).[5] The fifth path is the attainment of Buddhahood. The result is the attainment of the state of the two kāyas: dharmakāya (Tib. Chhos.sku) and the rūpakāya (Tib. gZugs.sku), which is the combination of sambhogakāya and nirmāṇakāya.

THE SIX VEHICLES OF THE DOCTRINE OF RESULT

THE THREE OUTER TANTRAS

1. According to the basic Kriyā tantra, the view is the realization that "all phenomena are without self-nature" (Chhos thams.chad ngo.bo.nyid med.pa rtogs). The activity is keeping clean and using the "three white things and three sweet things" (dKar.gsum mngar.gsum), and so on. The practice of meditation is to visualize oneself, the damtshig-sempa (samaya-sattva) as a subject, and the deity or yeshe-sempa (jñāna-sattva) in front of oneself like a king, and then to receive the blessings and siddhi from the wisdom deity. The path is to make offerings to the deity. The result is the attainment of the state of "vajra

---

5. The five paths are the path of accumulation (Tshogs.lam), the path of application (sByor.lam), the path of seeing (mThong.lam), the path of meditation (sGom.lam), and the path beyond practice (Mi.slob lam). In order to avoid misunderstanding, one should know that although both the Hīnayāna and Mahāyāna systems have what are called the "basis" and the "five paths," the meaning differs in these two systems. Also, within the Mahāyāna system, there are the "five paths" and the "ten stages," two ways of dividing the same progression, but with different names according to the different traditions.

holder of the three families" (Rigs.gsum rdo.rje 'dzin.pa'i sa)[6] in sixteen lifetimes.

2. According to the basic Upa tantra, the view is the "realization of the wisdom without self-nature" (Ngo.bo nyid med.pa'i shes.rab). The practice is mainly the same as in the Kriyā yoga. The meditation is to visualize oneself as the damtshig-sempa and to visualize the wisdom deity in front of oneself like a brother or a friend, and to receive blessings and siddhis from the wisdom deity. The result is the attainment of the state of the "vajra holder of the four families"[7] in seven lifetimes.

3. According to the basic Yoga tantra, the view is the realization that "all phenomena are free from all diffuse characteristics" (Chhos thams.chad spros.pa'i mtshan.ma thams.chad dang bral.ba). This is the view of "luminosity inseparable from great emptiness" ('Od.gsal stong.pa.nyid du lta). This is absolute truth. Relative truth is transmitted by the "realization of Dharmatā, that all phenomena are seen as the sphere of the Vajradhātu maṇḍala" (Kun rdzob chir snang tham.chad chhos.nyid rtogs.pa'i byin rlabs las rdo.rje dbyings kyi dkyil.'khor). The primary activity is the practice of the view or meditation, which is helped by the secondary activity of keeping clean. The practice of meditation is to visualize oneself as the damtshig-sempa and the wisdom deity in front of oneself; the wisdom deity, having been invited, merges into the damtshig-sempa like water being poured into water. The path is to meditate in this way on the "generative or visualizing phase"

6. Tathāgata or body family (sKu de.bzhin gshegs.pa'i rigs), lotus or speech family (gSung pad.ma'i rigs), and vajra or wisdom-mind family (Thugs rdo.rje rigs).

7. The fourth family is the jewel family of qualities (Yon.tan rin.chhen rigs).

(bsKyed.rim) of relative truth, and the "completive phase" (rDzogs.rim) of absolute truth. The result is the attainment of "vajra holder of the four families" in three lifetimes.

THE THREE INNER TANTRAS

There are three systems of meditation: "father tantra" (Pha.rgyud), "mother tantra" (Ma.rgyud), and the "nondual tantra" (gNyis.med.rgyud). Father tantra is predominantly the generative phase of visualizing the deity as being luminosity inseparable from great emptiness. Mother tantra is predominantly the completive phase of meditating on bliss inseparable from great emptiness. The nondual tantra is predominantly the meditation of the generative and completive phases in union. But according to the tradition of the Old School, these three are called Mahāyoga, Anuyoga, and Atiyoga.

4. The basic Mahāyoga view is to realize the "inseparability of phenomena, or appearance, and great emptiness" (sNang. stong dbyer.med). This is absolute truth. The skillful means to attain the inseparability of appearance and great emptiness is to meditate on everything as the pure appearance of the maṇḍala of deities. This is relative truth. The activity is the acceptance of the "five meats" and the "five nectars," and the nondifferentiation between dirty and clean. The result is the attainment of the state of maṇḍalas of five, one hundred, one thousand, or countless families in this lifetime or in the "in-between state" (Ba.rdo) after death.[8]

5. The basic Anuyoga view is to establish the three maṇḍalas: the "maṇḍala of Kuntuzangmo, the unborn dharmadhātu" (dByings skye.med kun.tu bzang.mo'i dkyil.'khor), whose

8. The fifth family is the Amoghasiddhi family of activity (Phrin.las don.yod grub.pa'i rigs). The hundred (etc.) families (Rigs.brgya'i khyab bdag) are contained in the five families (Tib. Rigs.lnga'i bdag.nyid). When the five skandhas are purified, they transform into the five Buddha families.

unobstructed skillful means of luminosity is the "maṇḍala of Kuntuzangpo, the yeshe wisdom" (Ye.shes kun.tu.bzang.po'i dkyil.'khor), and the inseparable union of these two is the "maṇḍala of Great Bliss, their son" (Sras bde.ba chhen.po'i dkyil.'khor). The activity is equanimity. The meditation is the practice of the "path of liberation" (Grol.lam), which is visualizing all phenomena and beings as the maṇḍala of deities, and the "path of skillful means" (Thabs.lam), such as the practice of the "sherab wisdom completive phase" (Shes.rab rdzogs.rim), or meditating on "channels, air, and essence" (rTsa, rLung, Thig.le). The inherent wisdom is developed by the path of skillful means. The result is the attainment of the "Body of Great Bliss" (dDe.ba chhen.po'i sku) in this lifetime.

6. The basis of the section of Upadesha or Precious Teachings of Atiyoga is to establish the view that all phenomena are spontaneously enlightened from the beginning. The activity is without acceptance or rejection: it is the recognition of all phenomena as the display of the dharmakāya. The practice is to establish dharmakāya wisdom, which is primordially pure, through the teaching of "the natural revelation of cutting through all substantial and insubstantial phenomena" (khregs.chhod) and to use the spontaneous wisdom of the sambhogakāya and the rainbow body of the nirmāṇakāya, which are "spontaneous luminosity" (Lhun.grub 'od.sal), through the teaching of "the natural revelation of passing spontaneously to the direct, clear light manifestation of buddhas" (Thod.rgal). Depending on the "six paths," the "four phenomena" arise in order. The result is the fulfillment of the "four confidences" (gDeng.bzhi). Since the result of Atiyoga is the realization that the spontaneous, perfect state of Kuntuzangpo exists right now, that there is nothing other than this, this is fulfillment or enlightenment. It is the recognition that saṃsāra is naturally nirvāna.

6

THE SUPERIORITIES OF MAHĀYĀNA AND VAJRAYĀNA

THERE ARE MANY WAYS IN which the Mahāyāna excels the Hīnayāna, all of which can be collected into seven great ways:

Great diligence (brTson.'grus chhen.po) is benefiting all sentient beings with great joy for countless kalpas.

Great intention (dMigs.pa chhen.po) is having not just an ordinary aim, but the aim of the Dharmatā, which is vast like the sky.

Great achievement (sGrub.pa chhen.po) is the achievement for the benefit of oneself and all sentient beings.

Great wisdom (Ye.shes chhen.po) is the realization of the two egoless states (bDag.med gnyis) and the wisdom of inseparable great emptiness and compassion which comes from this realization.

Great skillful means (Thabs.la mkhas.pa chhen.po) is remaining neither in saṃsāra nor in nirvāṇa, thus benefiting all sentient beings, including oneself.

Great fulfillment (sGrub.pa chhen.po) is the fulfillment of all the great qualities of the Buddha, including the ten strengths.

Great activity (Phrin.las chhen.po) is the spontaneous ability to benefit all sentient beings until saṃsāra is empty.

The doctrine of cause of the Hīnayāna and Mahāyāna and the doctrine of result of the Vajrayāna both teach the path to liberation, but there are four ways in which the doctrine of result is superior to the doctrine of cause. These four superiorities are as follows.

Without ignorance (Ma.rmongs.pa). The view of the doctrine of cause establishes the "absolute truth of the dharmatā" (Chhos.nyid don.dam bden.pa) establishing great emptiness free from all elaboration (sPros.pa thams.chad dang bral.ba stong.pa chhen.por gtan.la phab). The view of the doctrine of result establishes the "absolute truth of the dharmatā" as the "inseparable sphere of great emptiness and yeshe wisdom" (dByings dang ye.shes dbyer.med.pa). Because the view of the doctrine of cause excludes yeshe wisdom, the doctrine of result has the superiority of being without ignorance. In addition, the relative truth of the doctrine of cause is to establish all phenomena as being like an illusion or a dream. The relative truth of the doctrine of result is to establish all phenomena as being pure appearance and yeshe wisdom inseparable, and therefore has the superiority of being without ignorance.

Having many methods (Thabs.mang.ba). Although there are many methods of samādhi meditation in the doctrine of cause, none of the methods has the superior qualities of the Vajrayāna's generative and completive stages of visualization. If one has faith and preserves one's sacred Vajrayāna vow,[1] one can practice the samādhi meditation of generative and completive stages together.

Without hardships (dKa'.ba med.pa). According to the doc-

1. Sworn bonds with the guru and deities.

trine of cause, if "objects of desire" ('Dod.yon) are not abandoned, nirvāṇa cannot be attained. But according to the doctrine of result, if the method is skillful, nirvāṇa can be attained without abandoning the objects of desire. Therefore, the Vajrayāna has the superiority of being without hardships.

For those of keen faculties (dBang.po rnon.po). Those who follow the doctrine of cause have keener faculties than ordinary individuals, but those who follow the doctrine of result have superior faculties. Because they have "discerning insight," the sherab wisdom (Skt.prajñā; Tib. Shes.rab), they are not afraid of the deep view, and since they have essential faith in the Vajrayāna, they are never afraid of any kind of activity.

There are many ways in which Dzogchen Nyingthig excels the lower Vajrayāna, which can be collected into "five great ways"; however, these will not be explained here.

7

GREAT EMPTINESS

Although Hīnayāna, Mahāyāna, and Vajrayāna all use the same word, *voidness* or *great emptiness* (Skt. śunyatā; Tib. sTong.pa nyid), this word has different meanings in each yāna.

According to the Hīnayāna doctrines of the Vaibhāṣika (Bye.brag smra.ba) and Sautrāntika (mDo.sde.pa), the "self" (Gang.zag) is ego mind. Voidness is the "egolessness of the self" (Skt. Pudgala-nairātmya; Tib. Gang.zag.gi bdag.med). Generally, in Hīnayāna the term *Gang.zag.gi bdag.med* is used instead of *sTong.pa nyid*, although the latter is used in some of the śastras.

All the teachings of the Mahāyāna are contained in the two teachings of the Yogācāra (Sems.tsam.pa), or "just mind" doctrine, and Mādhyamika (dBu.ma.pa), or the "middle way."

According to the Yogācāra, voidness is the voidness of both the "object grasped" (gZung.ba yul), and the "mind which grasps the object" ('Dzin.pa sems). Within the Yogācāra (Sems.tsam.pa), there are two divisions: Sems.tsam rnam bden.pa and Sems.tsam rnam brdzun.pa. According to Sems.tsam rnam bden.pa, all various outer phenomena and consciousness are true aspects of the mind. According to "Sems.tsam rnam brdzun.pa," all various outer phenomena are deluded habits, and consciousness is not true because the mind is deluded; the self-nature of both phenomena and consciousness is delusion.

Within Mādhyamika, there are the two divisions of dBu.ma rang.rgyud.pa and dBu.ma thal.'gyur.ba.

According to the dBu.ma rang.rgyud.pa, both the various outer phenomena and the mind which perceives these aspects are not real, they are just appearance. Absolute reality is that there is no inherent essence to the mind which knows.

According to the dBu.ma thal.'gyur.ba, voidness is the emptiness of "the four or eight extremes" (mTha' bzhi 'am brgyad). According to this system, all phenomena arise from "interconnection" (rTen.'brel) and are "free from the activities of the four or eight extremes" (mTha' bzhi 'am brgyad kyi spros.pa dang bral.ba).

The four extremes are: not permanent, not not-permanent, not existing, not not-existing.

The eight extremes are: unobstructed, unborn, unceasing, not permanent, not coming, not going, having meanings which are not distinct or separate, having meanings which are not not-distinct or separate. Being free from the activities of the four or eight extremes is voidness.

According to Nyingmapa Vajrayāna teachings, there are three main practices: Mahāyoga, Anuyoga, and Atiyoga.

The main practice of Mahāyoga is the practice of the "generative phase" (bsKyed.rim) and "completive phase" (rDzogs. rim) meditation on "great emptiness inseparable from luminosity" (gSal.stong). Great emptiness, according to Mahāyoga, is the great emptiness of luminosity. The main practice of Anuyoga is the meditation on "great emptiness inseparable from bliss" (bDe.stong). Great emptiness, according to Anuyoga, is the great emptiness of bliss. The main practice of Atiyoga is the meditation on "great emptiness inseparable from natural mind or awareness" (Rig.stong). Great emptiness, according to Atiyoga, is the great emptiness of natural mind or awareness.

8

THE TWO TRUTHS

THE SPACE OF APPEARANCE, OR dharmadhātu, is free from all conceptualization, so there is no basis to the "two truths" (bDen.pa gnyis). However, not all beings recognize this state which is free from conceptualization. In order to help beings recognize it, the Buddha distinguished between those with deluded and undeluded minds by explaining the two truths: relative truth (Kun.rdzob bden.pa)[1] and absolute truth (Don.dam bden.pa).[2]

In order to accommodate the differences in the minds of individuals, the Buddha explained the two truths according to different systems.

According to the general Hīnayāna, relative truth is all phenomena, including the gross phenomena of the five skandhas. Absolute truth is the realization which comes from examining the five skandhas to find where the self or ego dwells. By examining, one realizes that this ego does not dwell anywhere, that it does not exist, and that the mind and all phenomena are composed of instantaneous indivisible particles.[3] This is absolute truth according to the general Hīnayāna.

According to the Sautrāntika (mDo.sde.pa) school[4] of the

1. *Kun*: all; *rdzob*: deceive or conceal; *Kun.rdzob*: conditional or relative; *bden.pa*: truth.

2. *Don*: purpose, meaning; *dam.pa*: undeceived; *bden.pa*: truth

3. See chapter 5.

4. See chapter 3, note 2.

Hīnayāna, relative truth is that objects do not function. Absolute truth is the essence of the functioning of phenomena.

According to the Yogācāra (Sems.tsam.pa) school[5] of the Mahāyāna, relative truth is parikalpita (Kun.brtag) and paratantra (gZhan.dbang). Absolute truth is parinişpanna (Yongs.grub).

According to Patrul Rinpoche, relative truth is deluded mind and its objects, and absolute truth is what is beyond body, speech, and mind.

According to Mipham Rinpoche, within relative truth, the body can function, speech can be spoken, and the mind can understand. Within absolute truth, bodies are beyond function, speech is beyond expression, and the mind is beyond cognitive thought.

There are many other explanations of the two truths which will not be given here. One should examine the various systems carefully and decide which of them one wishes to follow.

The following is a brief explanation of the two truths of the Mahāyāna according to general Mādhyamika and higher Mādhyamika, and also according to the Vajrayāna.

1. GENERAL MĀDHYAMIKA

The essence of relative truth according to general Mādhyamika is the deluded mind and all phenomena which are the objects of deluded mind; it is whatever is true for the deluded mind.

According to this system, there are two divisions of relative truth: "inverted relative truth" (Log.pa'i kun.rdzob), which does not function, like the reflection of the moon in water, and

5. See chapter 3, note 2, and chapter 7.

"actual relative truth" (Yang.dag kun.rdzob), which is like the moon in the sky, which can shine and illuminate the darkness.

According to general Mādhyamika, actual relative truth has four characteristics. It is:

Collectively perceived (mThun.par snang.ba): For example, water, fire, sun, and moon are perceived similarly by everyone;

Capable of effect or function (Don.byed nus.pa): For example, the earth can support all human beings;

Produced by root cause and condition (rGyu.rkyen gyis skyes.pa): For example, when a seed, which is the root cause, and water, warmth, and air, which are the contributing circumstances, come together, a plant grows; and

Nonexistent when examined (brTag na dben.pa).

The absolute truth according to the lower Svātantrika school (Rang.rgyud 'og.ma) of general Mādhyamika is "self-awareness wisdom" (Rang.rig.pa'i ye.shes). This is the realization that there is neither subject nor object. All is beyond thought or speech; all is just like a mirage.

2. HIGHER MĀDHYAMIKA

Inverted relative truth according to higher Mādhyamika is all individual viewpoints and the conceptual doctrines of nihilists and substantialists. These are inverted relative truth because they do not function for the abandonment of saṃsāra and the attainment of nirvāṇa.

According to this view, all personal phenomena are inverted relative truth. For example, when a person doing devotional practice is in an unrealized state, all phenomena arise as inverted relative truth. But from the attainment of the first state of bodhisattvahood onward, during both actual meditation and after-meditation's phenomena, all arises as actual relative truth because all is unobstructed and is realized as illusion.

According to higher Mādhyamika, actual relative truth also has four characteristics. It is:

Collectively perceived, like the eight examples of māyā: magic, a dream, a bubble, a rainbow, lightning, the moon reflected in water, a mirage, and a city of celestial musicians (gandharvas);

Capable of effect or function, because with the realization that all phenomena are like the eight examples of māyā, saṃsāra can be abandoned and nirvāṇa can be attained;

Produced by root cause and conditions because of the realization of the illusory nature of phenomena. The root cause of this realization is the two accumulations of merit and wisdom. The contributing circumstance, or necessary condition, is the teachings of the precious teacher; and

Nonexistent when examined because actually there is not even illusion; all phenomena, existence, nonexistence, truth, and untruth are great emptiness.

According to this view, the essence of absolute truth (Don.dam bden.pa)[6] is the dharmadhātu which is beyond all activity. Within absolute truth there are no distinctions because absolute truth is free from all mental activity. Sublime beings have the true realization that the essential characteristic of absolute truth is freedom from all mental activity, while ordinary philosophers and people who do not have this realization

6. The literal meaning of absolute truth (Don.dam bden.pa) is as follows. *Don* means purpose; the purpose is the attainment of liberation. *Dam.pa* means undeceived; with a good understanding of the nature of the mind, one is never deceived. *bDen.pa* means truth; the mind which is not mistaken, the natural mind which is undeluded and unchanging, is always true.

only guess at the meaning of absolute truth. For this reason, the Buddha taught two systems of absolute truth:

The absolute truth of enumeration (rNam.grangs don.dam bden.pa). According to the higher Svātantrika school (Rang. rgyud gong.ma), absolute truth is not explained by saying that all is just like a mirage. Although there is really no truth to relative truth because absolute truth does not exist anywhere, in this system absolute truth can still be explained in relative terms as the absolute truth of enumeration by listing things as being great emptiness. For example: "Form is great emptiness, great emptiness is form, great emptiness is not different from form, form is not different from great emptiness." In the same way that form is explained, the other skandhas of feeling, perception, intention, and consciousness are explained. All together, these are called the "sixteen great emptinesses."

The absolute truth without enumeration (rNam.grangs ma. yin.pa'i don.dam bden.pa). This system explains that the basis of understanding the nature of all phenomena is that it is separate from all activity, and that the wisdom of the Buddha is free from all enumeration.

According to the Prāsaṅgika (Thal.'gyur.ba) school of highest Mādhyamika, in actual meditation, the absolute truth which is free from all mental activity is neither "absolute truth of enumeration" nor "absolute truth without enumeration"; there is no promise that absolute truth is anything.

Briefly, relative truth and absolute truth can be explained as follows.

Inverted relative truth. This is the ordinary state of the individual who maintains with attachment the point of view that all phenomena are real, not illusory. For example, the mirage of a beautiful actress created by a magician, to which the onlookers become attached, believing it is real, is like the phenomena which arise in one's mind to which one becomes attached, believing they are real. This is an example of the view of the ordinary individual.

Actual relative truth. This is the sublime state of the realization of the illusory nature of all phenomena. With this realization, all attachment to phenomena as being real vanishes, but in one's practice, there is still some attachment to this illusion because of previous habit. As one's practice becomes higher, even though there is still illusion, one's attachment to the illusion becomes less and less. For example, as the magician in a magic show is not attached to the beautiful actress whom he creates, so even if phenomena arise in the mind of a sublime being, there is no attachment to these phenomena as being real. This is the example of the view of the sublime being.

Absolute truth. This is the state of buddhahood in which there are neither phenomena nor absence of phenomena; neither conception of attachment nor of nonattachment. For example, one who is not affected by the apparitions, mirages, or mantras of the magician is like a buddha for whom there is neither attachment nor nonattachment. This is the example of the stage of buddhahood.

To summarize, absolute truth is the firm realization of the basic condition of the dharmatā, the realization that all phenomena are beyond existing and not existing, eternalism and nihilism, being true or false, beyond all activity, and are free from the two extremes of knowing and not knowing.

The Prajñāpāramitā, the two truths of higher Mādhyamika, etc., all teach that relative truth is inseparable from absolute truth and absolute truth is inseparable from relative truth; in reality, there is only one truth.

For the Buddha's wisdom mind, there is no difference between object and subject, but because the wisdom mind of ordinary individuals is obscured, we must practice systematically. We must understand that the basic condition of all phenomena is illusion. We must realize that actually it neither exists nor does not exist, but is like the sky. The understanding that ultimately the two truths are inseparable is the relative truth which is understood by the sublime mind.

The self-nature of the mind which understands relative truth is absolute truth, because if we examine the nature of the thoughts which arise in the mind, we will see that they do not exist anywhere: they neither exist nor do not exist, they are unobstructed, unborn, unceasing, not permanent, not coming, not going, their meanings are not distinct or separate, their meanings are not nondistinct or nonseparate: they are completely beyond all activity. This is the dharmatā, and this dharmatā is the absolute truth. Outside, inside, shape, color, etc., do not exist anywhere; all is like the sky.

Whoever realizes actual relative truth also realizes absolute truth, because actual relative truth and absolute truth are inseparable. Ultimately, there are not two truths, because in Dharmadhātu there is no basis for expression of the two truths. Buddhahood is Wisdom Mind within which there is no dualistic mind. Where there is no dualistic mind, there are no two truths. When we remain in natural Wisdom Mind or awareness of inseparable great emptiness and luminosity, there are not two truths, because this is Dharmadhātu.

3. VAJRAYĀNA

According to the higher Vajrayāna, inverted relative truth is attachment to all phenomena as being ordinary reality. Actual relative truth is seeing all phenomena as transformed into wisdom deities and their purelands by visualizing or meditating. Thus, all phenomena cannot go beyond the great empty expanse of the Dharmadhātu: this is absolute truth.

9

THE TRIPIṬAKA AND THE THREE TRAININGS

TO EXPLAIN THE BUDDHA'S teachings according to meaning, it is said that the Buddha taught the two truths; to explain his teachings in terms of time, it is said that the Buddha turned the Wheel of Dharma three times; and to explain his teachings in terms of antidote, it is said that the Buddha taught the Tripiṭaka (sDe.snod gsum), or the three sections of the "Dharma of precept" (Lung.gi chhos).

The Tripiṭaka, or three sections of the Dharma of precept, are:

The *vinaya* ('Dul.ba'i sde.snod), which is predominantly the antidote for desire;

The *sūtra* (mDo.sde'i sde.snod), which is predominantly the antidote for anger; and

The *abhidharma* (mNgon.pa'i sde.snod), which is predominantly the antidote for ignorance.[1]

According to the Vajrayāna, there is also the wisdom-holders' tantric section (Rig.'dzin sngags kyi sde snod).

The "three trainings" (bsLab.pa gsum) are the three sections of the "Dharma of realization" (rTogs.pa'i chhos):

---

1. The antidotes of all three passions are also contained within each of the antidotes.

Morality training (Tshul.khrims kyi bslab.pa);
Samādhi training (Ting.nge 'dzin.gyi bslab.pa); and
Prajñā training (Shes.rab kyi bslab.pa).

In general, the vinaya teaching is mainly the explanation of the morality training, the sūtra teaching is mainly the explanation of the samādhi training, and the abhidharma teaching is mainly the explanation of the prajñā wisdom training.

The teachings of the Tripiṭaka and the three trainings are all contained within each yāna.

According to the Hīnayāna, vinaya is all the teachings about discipline, such as the two hundred and fifty monastic vows of a monk. When the meaning of the vinaya is realized, the practice is the morality training. Sūtra is the teaching about meditation on the "disgusting things," etc. When this teaching is realized, the practice is the samādhi training of śamatha and vipaśyanā. Abhidharma is the teaching on the egolessness of self. When this teaching is realized, the practice is the prajñā wisdom training.

According to the Mahāyāna, vinaya is the many distinctive teachings on the root downfalls from the bodhisattva vow. When these teachings are realized, the practice is the morality training. Sūtra is the teachings on as many entrances as possible into samādhi. When these teachings are realized, the practice is the samādhi training. Abhidharma is the many distinctive or essential teachings on great emptiness, and when these teachings are realized, the practice is the prajñā wisdom training.

According to the Vajrayāna, vinaya is the teaching of the "tantric promise" (Skt. samaya; Tib.Dam.tshig). The Vajrayāna damtshig is to practice seeing all phenomena as pure. When this teaching is realized, the practice is the morality training. Sūtra is the teachings of the visualization of the generative and completive stages of meditation. When these teachings are realized, the practice is the samādhi training. Abhidharma is the teachings of the Great Perfection (rDzogs.pa Chhen.po). When these teachings are realized, the practice is the prajñā wisdom training.

10

DHARMA OF PRECEPT AND DHARMA OF REALIZATION

All sacred Dharma can be collected into Dharma of Precept (Lung.gi chhos) and Dharma of Realization (rTogs.pa'i chhos).[1]

Dharma of Precept

Within Dharma of precept, there are two sections: the Buddha's Speech (Skt. vacana; Tib. bKa') and Followers' Speech (bsTan.bchos).

Within the Buddha's Speech section, there are the following three categories:

1. Speech that comes from the Buddha (Zhal nas gsungs.pa'i bka'): According to sūtra, this means the words spoken directly by the Buddha Śākyamuni. According to tantra, it means the speech of Vajradhara (rDo.rje 'Chang).
2. Speech transmitted by the Buddha's blessing (Byin. gyis.brlabs.pa'i bka'): There are five sections within this category: speech transmitted by the blessings of the Buddha's body, speech, wisdom mind, qualities, and activities. These are best explained by examples:

   Speech transmitted by the blessing of the Buddha's

1. See chapter 9.

body: Once, the Buddha placed his hand on the head of his disciple Dorje Nyingpo (Vajragarbha). Although the Buddha did not give him any oral teaching, on receiving this blessing Dorje Nyingpo was able to give teachings to others on the "Sūtra of the Ten Stages" (mDo.sde sa.bchu.pa).

Speech transmitted by the blessing of the Buddha's speech: Although Gyalpo Makyedra (King Ajātaśatru) committed many bad deeds, he repented of them, so the Buddha told Mañjuśrī to purify the king of his regret and the bad karma of these deeds. It then appeared as if Mañjuśrī gave blessings and teachings to the king, but these blessings actually originated from the Buddha.

Speech transmitted by the blessing of the Buddha's wisdom mind: Once, while the Buddha was in samādhi, he bestowed the blessing of his wisdom mind on Śāriputra and Avalokiteśvara. By this blessing, they were able to teach the *Heart Sutra* to each other.

Speech transmitted by the blessing of the Buddha's qualities and activities: If one has a connection with them, all sounds, whether they come from birds, flowers, rocks, trees, wind, the sky, a large drum of the gods, or from anywhere, are the blessings of the Dharma's sound.

3. Speech that has the Buddha's assent (rJes.su gnang.ba'i bka'): The Buddha said that any teachings given after his passing away that were not against or opposite the teachings of the vinaya, sūtra, and abhidharma must be accepted as being the same as the Buddha's speech.

Follower's Speech is the explanation of the intention of the Buddha's speech. There are three categories of authors of follower's speech. The superior authors are the spiritual authorities who have realized the truth of dharmatā. They are superior because, through understanding the nature of dharmatā, they do not make mistakes in their explanation. The intermediate authors are those who have beheld the face of the yidam and have the yidam's sanction, or the sanction of the teacher of their lineage, to write follower's speech. The lesser authors must at least have knowledge of the "five branches of science" (Rig.pa'i gnas lnga), which are art (bZo), medicine (gSo.ba), philology (sGra),[2] logic (Tshad.ma), and philosophy (Nang.don rig.pa).[3]

Vasubandhu (dByig.gnyen), who was the brother of Asaṅga (Thogs.med), stated in his *rNam.bshad rig.pa:*

> Follower's speech is whatever amends or corrects all the enemies of the passions, without exception, and protects from the lower realms of existence. If it has the qualities of amending and protecting, then it is follower's speech. It is also separate from the impurities of the "six outside" [non-Buddhist] doctrines, which are: being without meaning, having opposite meaning, only heard (and not practiced), being only for debate, being harmful to sentient beings, and being without compassion.
>
> Follower's speech also completely contains the "three superior essential characteristics of Buddhist Dharma": accomplishing the temporary and perpetual great meaning, abandoning saṃsāra, and attaining nirvāṇa.

DHARMA OF REALIZATION

This is the realization which comes from the practice of the Dharma of precept. For example, according to the Hīnayāna

---

2. Within philology there are the four subdivisions of poetics: metaphor (sNyan.ngag), composition (sDeb.sbyor), synonyms (mNgon.brjod), and astrology (sKar.rtsis).

3. In all three yānas, wherever there is the teaching of the view, meditation, and activity, it is philosophy.

path, the Dharma of precept is the teaching of the moral discipline, and the Dharma of realization is the realization of the state of egolessness of self. According to the Mahāyāna path, the Dharma of precept is the teaching of bodhicitta, and the Dharma of realization is the realization of the two selfless states. According to the Vajrayāna path, the Dharma of precept is the teaching of the pure maṇḍala visualization, and the Dharma of realization is the realization that all phenomena of the mind become wisdom inseparable from pure maṇḍala.

All Dharma writing, speech, and sound are the Dharma of precept and all Dharma meanings are the Dharma of realization. For example, if people receive the teaching not to kill and then become ashamed of killing, this is the Dharma of precept. When they realize this teaching and cease to kill, this is the Dharma of realization. If one receives the teaching to meditate on the meaning of the mind, this is the Dharma of precept. When one realizes this meditation and comes to understand the nature of the mind and practices this realization, this is the Dharma of realization. In brief, all Dharma teachings are the Dharma of precept. Whoever realizes the Dharma of precept has the Dharma of realization, because the Dharma of realization is the realization of all teachings.

One needs a boat to cross a river, even though one leaves the boat behind once the other shore has been reached. In the same way, we now need both the Dharma of precept and the Dharma of realization until we finally attain the state of dharmakāya. At the beginning, the teaching of the Dharma of precept is necessary because the Dharma of realization comes from it. As the Dharma of realization becomes higher and higher, the dependence on the Dharma of precept becomes less and less. When the Dharma of precept is realized, the meaning of the Dharma of precept dissolves into the Dharma of realization. Then the Dharma of realization expands and increases, and as new

Dharma of realization comes, wisdom becomes more powerful, and the previous Dharma of realization made by the ordinary intellect automatically vanishes as ordinary intellect vanishes. Finally, when the state of dharmakāya is attained, the Dharma of precept automatically vanishes and the Dharma of realization becomes perfect.

In the Mahāyāna system, after the tenth bodhisattva stage, there is the eleventh stage and then the realization of the dharmakāya. Before this, the Dharma of precept and the Dharma of realization are different. Then, through practicing and through not going from stage to stage, all gradually becomes the dharmakāya, or the body of Dharma, within nondualistic Wisdom Mind's one taste. But according to highest inner tantric teaching, whoever is really doubtless cannot from the beginning separate Dharma of precept from Dharma of realization since, from the beginning, basis and result are pure. There is no differentiation between the aspect of Buddha's display and the aspect of his followers' display since all is the same Wisdom Mind, without separation. The path is only named momentarily for recognition.

Since, from the beginning, basis and result are inseparable, wisdom appearance—which is wisdom body, wisdom speech, wisdom mind, wisdom quality, and wisdom activity—increases timelessly, directionlessly, and unendingly, so there is not even the name of exhaustible precept Dharma or recognizable realization of Dharma.

According to sūtra, the volumes of Dharma are the symbols of the Dharma of precept, representing the Buddha's speech. According to tantra, the volumes of Dharma and the sound of Dharma are the symbols of the Dharma of precept and the phenomena of Dharma are the symbols of the Dharma of realization.

II

THE FOUR OBSCURATIONS

THE FOUR OBSCURATIONS (sGrib.pa bzhi) are the karmic obscuration (Las.kyi sgrib.pa), the obscuration of passions (Nyon.mongs.kyi sgrib.pa), the intellectual obscuration, or obscuration of not knowing (Shes.bya'i sgrib.pa), and the obscuration of habit (Bag.chhags kyi sgrib.pa).

Karmic obscuration comes from committing any of countless unvirtuous deeds, which may be summarized as the five inexpiable sins (mTshams.med lnga), the ten unvirtuous deeds (Mi.dge.ba bchu), the breaking of the various vows (samaya) of the Hīnayāna, Mahāyāna, and Vajrayāna, etc. The attainment of a precious body such as that of a god or human is obstructed by karmic obscuration.

Obscuration by the countless passions or emotions can be condensed into the obscuration of the five passions,[1] the obscuration of the three passions,[2] or the obscuration of ego. The states of attainment for Hīnayāna practitioners are obstructed by the obscuration of the passions.

The obscuration of not knowing is the "threefold sphere" ('Khor gsum), which is the three concomitants of object, subject, and action. The obscuration of habit, according to sūtra, is a very subtle form of the obscuration of not knowing.

1. Desire, anger, ignorance, jealousy, and pride.
2. Desire, anger, and ignorance.

According to tantra, it is the basis of "habit inherent in the three phenomena of body, speech, and mind" (sNang gsum 'pho.ba'i bag.chhags), which is also a very subtle obscuration. This obscuration of habit is the cause, latent residue, or habit of the white phenomenon, or subtle seed, which gives rise to the body; the cause, latent residue, or habit of the red phenomenon, or subtle seed, which gives rise to speech; and the cause, latent residue, or habit of the vital air, which gives rise to the mind. Freedom from the obstructions of the obscuration of not knowing and the obscuration of habit is the "state of omniscient wisdom" (rNam.pa thams.chad mkhyen.pa'i ye.shes).

12

EMPOWERMENT

ACCORDING TO THE TANTRIC system, the purpose of empowerment (dBang) is to receive blessings and power. Many tantras reveal that if empowerment is not received, accomplishment (Skt. siddhi; Tib. dNgos.grub) will never be attained. As it is said, "However much sand is pressed, oil will never come." For example, even though a prince is the son of a king, if he never ascends the throne, he will have no power to work for his own benefit or for the benefit of his subjects. Without empowerment, one has no lineage, and it is not possible to practice for one's own benefit or to teach for the benefit of others. If we receive an empowerment, we have the blessing and power to practice, and can then teach others.

The essence and root cause of buddhahood is within everyone. However, without the necessary condition of meeting a teacher who has the wisdom and the blessing of lineage, this essence of buddhahood will never blossom. For example, even if a seed is planted in the earth, without the necessary condition of warmth, moisture, or fertilizer, the seed will not grow. It will only grow with these good circumstances. The essence of buddhahood is like this seed, and when the connection occurs between this seed and the teacher who has wisdom and blessing, buddhahood blossoms.

According to the doctrine of cause of the Hīnayāna view, we

must purify obscurations and accumulate merit for countless aeons in order to attain buddhahood. Empowerment is important because, if we have faith and can practice the Vajrayāna path, by receiving the blessing of empowerment from the teacher (bLa.ma), our obscurations are purified. Then we can recognize through our teacher that, from the beginning, the true nature of our own wisdom is the three kāyas, and we can attain buddhahood in one lifetime.

But if the teacher does not have wisdom and blessing, then even though the true nature of our wisdom is the three kāyas, we will not be able to recognize this perfectly. Therefore, it is more important that the teacher has the wisdom and the blessing of a lineage than worldly power and fame. If he does have the wisdom and blessing, it is important that disciples who are receiving the empowerment have faith without any doubt in the teacher and in the tantric teaching. In whatever form the teacher appears, whether he is a layman or a monk, humble or great, if he has the blessings of wisdom and qualities, then he is qualified to bestow empowerments. There are many kinds of empowerments or initiations.

The empowerments of the outer tantras are:

The three empowerments of Kriyā tantra

1. Nectar empowerment (Chhu dbang) or vase empowerment (Bum.pa'i dbang),
2. Crown empowerment (Chod.pan. gyi dbang), and
3. Name empowerment (Ming. gi dbang).

The empowerments of the Upa tantra, which include the three empowerments of Kriyā tantra plus

4. Vajra empowerment (rDo.rje dbang), and

5. Bell empowerment (Dril.bu'i dbang).[1]

The empowerments of Yoga tantra, which include the five empowerments of Kriyā tantra and Upa tantra plus

6. Vajra master empowerment (rDo.rje slob.dpon dbang).

The empowerments of the inner tantras are:

The empowerments of Mahāyoga:

1. The outer ten beneficent empowerments (Phyi phan.pa'i dbang bchu), which include the "four basic empowerments" (dBang bzhi),
2. The inner five enabling empowerments (Nang nus.pa'i dbang lnga), and
3. The three secret profound empowerments (gSang.ba zab.mo'i dbang gsum).

The empowerments of Anuyoga:

1. The thirty-six basic empowerments (rTsa.ba'i dbang sum.chu.so.drug.), which include:

   Outer empowerment (Phyi.yi dbang),
   Inner empowerment (Nang.gi dbang),
   Sādhana empowerment (sGrub.pa'i dbang),
   Secret empowerment (gSang.ba'i dbang), and

2. The eight hundred and thirty-one branch empowerments (Yan.lag.gi dbang).

The four empowerments of Atiyoga:

1. Elaborate empowerment (sPros.bchas dbang),
2. Unelaborate empowerment (sPros.med dbang),

1. These five empowerments together are called "Rig.pa'i dbang lnga."

3. Very unelaborate empowerment (Shin.tu spros. med dbang), and
4. Extremely unelaborate empowerment (Rab.tu spros.med dbang).

Extensive empowerments have two parts: the preparation and the main body. Various symbolic articles are employed, according to the various kinds of empowerments. No explanation of these empowerments will be given here, but when one receives lower and higher empowerments, if one listens carefully to the lama, their meanings will become clear.

The following is a brief explanation of the four empowerments of higher tantra.

The usual system for the empowerment of outer tantra is the vase empowerment (Bum dbang). The usual system for the empowerment in the inner tantra is the four basic empowerments (dBang. bzhi) which includes the vase empowerment and the "three superior empowerments" (dBang gong.ma gsum), which are: the "secret empowerment" (gSang dbang), the "prajñā-jñāna wisdom empowerment" (Shes.rab ye.shes. kyi dbang), and the "word empowerment" (Tshig dbang).

It is only through the blessings of the four kāyas of the lama that we can receive the empowerment which enables us to quickly reach buddhahood in order to benefit all sentient beings.

The empowerments from the four kāyas of the lama are received as follows.

The vase empowerment is bestowed by the nirmāṇakāya lama. The wisdom deity is emanated from the lama and bestows the empowerment. When receiving the vase empowerment, we must first visualize the wisdom deity in his maṇḍala. Outwardly, the vase is the symbol for the palace of the wisdom deity, and the wisdom deity dwells within this vase. The lama's body is visualized as the essence of the maṇḍala of the wisdom deity, and our own body is visualized as the damtshigpa.[2] Then the lama, who is the wisdom deity, merges into the vase, the vase is placed on the crown of our head, and the wisdom deity dissolves into us as we drink the nectar from the vase. From beginningless time until now, we have accumulated "countless obscurations of ripened karma" (rNam.smin.gyi sgrib.pa) as well as "obscurations of the body and the veins or channels" (Lus rtsa.yi sgrib.pa) by committing the "ten unvirtuous actions" and the "five inexpiable sins," which cause the "obscuration of karma."[3] These are purified by the vase empowerment, by which we receive the blessing of the body of the wisdom deity. Then we become inseparable with the body of the wisdom deity, and the remainder of the nectar flows up in the body and overflows at the top of the head, where it is transformed into the crown of the five buddhas. By this, we are empowered to practice the generative stage of the visualization of the deity, and with this good opportunity, we can attain nirmāṇakāya.

The secret empowerment is bestowed by the sambhogakāya lama yab-yum. From the secret place of the sambhogakāya lama yab-yum, bodhicitta nectar (Skt. amṛta; Tib. bDud.rtsi) flows, and by tasting this nectar the "obcurations of the passions" (Nyon.mongs.kyi sgrib.pa)[4] and the "obscurations of the vital air of speech" (Ngag rlung. gi sgrib.pa) which we have accumulated from beginningless time until now are purified. Sometimes, during the secret empowerment, the rosary of the mantra is at the lama's throat center. Light streams from this mantra and is absorbed into our own throat center. By receiving

2. For example, if one receives Dorje Sempa's initiation, one should visualize the lama as Dorje Sempa's wisdom body in his maṇḍala.

3. See chapter 11.

4. See chapter 11.

the secret empowerment, we are empowered to practice the completive stage and meditation on the channels, air, and essence (Skt. prāṇa, nāḍī, bindu; Tib. rTsa, rLung, Thig.le), which includes recitation of the mantra. With this good opportunity we can attain sambhogakāya.

The wisdom empowerment is bestowed by the dharmakāya lama. The lama emanates his wisdom consort (Rig.ma) in order to bestow her upon us. We visualize ourselves as the wisdom deity and unite with the wisdom consort. Then the wisdom of "bliss-emptiness inseparable from beginningless time until now" (bDe.stong lhan.chig skyes. pa'i ye.shes) arises and is experienced. Thus, the "obscurations of not knowing" (Shes.bya'i sgrib.pa)[5] and the "obscurations of the mind bindu" (Yid thig.le'i sgrib.pa) are purified. In some systems, in the wisdom empowerment, the lama places a dorje, or other symbols according to the particular sādhana, at our heart center as a gesture, and this is absorbed within. By receiving the wisdom empowerment, we are empowered to practice the sherab-yeshe wisdom, and with this good opportunity, we can attain the state of dharmakāya.

The word empowerment is bestowed by the "Essence kāya" (Skt. svabhāvikakāya; Tib. Ngo.bo nyid sku) lama. The lama indicates to us by words in order to make us realize that the basis of our own natural mind is Buddha nature. Thus, the "obscurations of habits" (Bag.chhags.kyi sgrib.pa) resulting from "subject-object duality" (gZung.'dzin), which we have accumulated from beginningless time until now, are purified.

In some systems, in the word empowerment, the lama indicates by a gesture, such as showing an object like a crystal, and explains how we should watch our mind. Then he says: "When you observe the crystal, you will see that its essence is great

5. See chapter 11.

emptiness, but it is not only great emptiness, because many rainbows emanate unobstructedly from it. In the same way, the three kāyas are contained within our Wisdom Mind. The nature of Wisdom Mind is great emptiness, dharmakāya. But, it is not only great emptiness, it is also luminous sambhogakāya and unobstructed nirmāṇakāya. These inseparable three kāyas are altogether the Essence kāya. All the maṇḍalas of the buddhas (rGyal.ba'i dkyil'khor) arise from the three kāyas, and the three kāyas come from your Wisdom Mind."

Then we are empowered to practice the inseparable "primordially pure emptiness" (Ka.dag. stong.pa nyid) and "spontaneous luminosity" (Lhun.grub 'od.gsal), and with this good opportunity, we can attain the Essence kāya.

All the countless buddhas are contained in the three kāyas or the four kāyas, and these are contained in the lama. The empowerment which we take from our root lama is called the "basis empowerment" (gZhi dbang). When we practice the sādhana, we take the empowerment from the maṇḍala in front of us. This is called the "path empowerment" (Lam.gyi dbang). As a consequence of receiving the outer blessings of the three or four kāyas in the basis empowerment or path empowerment, the inner state of the three or the four kāyas which is our own basic self-nature or Wisdom Mind becomes very powerful and is perfected. This is called the "result empowerment" ('Bras.bu'i dbang).

13

THE OBJECT OF REFUGE

IN BUDDHISM, THE OBJECT OR place of refuge is the outer Three Jewels (dKon.mchhog gsum), the inner Three Roots (rTsa.ba gsum), and the secret Three Kāyas (sKu gsum).

1. The "Three Jewels" are the Buddha, the Dharma, and the Saṅgha.

Buddha in Tibetan is *Sangs.rgyas. Sangs* means dispelled: the Buddha has completely dispelled all ignorance and has awakened from the sleep of ignorance. *rGyas* means increase or expand: the Buddha has measurelessly expanded all wisdom infallible qualities.

Dharma in Tibetan is *Chhos.* In general, *Chhos* means all kinds of phenomena. According to worldly ego, *Chhos* means all phenomena which cause saṃsāra. But in this case, Chhos is the antidote to saṃsāra and consists of all spiritual wisdom appearance. According to the Mahāyāna and Vajrayāna, Dharma is the Buddha's teaching of the "path to liberation" (Lam.gi chhos), which includes the Dharma of precept and the Dharma of realization, as explained in chapter 10. In particular, for the Vajrayāna, Dharma includes the "Dharma of result" ('Bras.bu'i chhos) which is the complete purification of perceptions so that all appearances are the Buddha's body, speech, mind, qualities, and activities, and the maṇḍala of the deities, buddhafields, etc. All these results are attained with the realization of the Vajrayāna teachings.

Saṅgha in Tibetan is *dGe.'dun. dGe* means virtue. *'Dun* means to strive toward one-pointedly. The Saṅgha are those who practice virtue on the path of Dharma. There are two kinds of saṅgha: the saṅgha of ordinary individuals (So.so'i skye.bo'i dge.'dun) and the saṅgha of sublime beings ('Phags.pa'i dge.'dun). The saṅgha of ordinary individuals are those who practice the path of accumulation (Tshogs lam) and the path of application (sByor lam). The sublime saṅgha are those who practice the path of seeing (mThong lam), which is the realization of the truth of dharmatā or natural mind, the path of development or meditation (sGom lam) and the path beyond practice (Mi.slob lam), which means all study or teaching and practice have been exhausted, as they are no longer necessary. There are two systems of explaining the path beyond practice: one system says that it is the final path to reach buddhahood; the other says that it is buddhahood itself, and there is no longer any path.

The saṅgha who follow the Mahāyāna path are called the general outer saṅgha (Thun.mong phyi.yi dge.'dun). The saṅgha who practice the Vajrayāna teaching are called the extraordinary inner saṅgha (Thun.min nang.gi dge. 'dun), or inner Vidyādhara saṅgha (Rig.'dzin nang.gi dge.'dun).

2. The Three Roots are the lama, the yidam, and the khadro.

Lama (guru): *La* means that which is most precious, life itself. "Ma" means mother. Just as a mother has great love and compassion for her children, and acts with this love and compassion for their benefit, so the lama acts with unobstructed compassion to benefit all sentient beings.

Yidam (deva): *Yid* means mind. *Dam* means an inseparable bond through pure samaya. According to the minds of all individual practitioners, there is a special deity with whom they have an inseparable connection.

Khadro (ḍākinī; Tib. mKha'.'dro): *mKha'* means sky; not the ordinary sky, but the sky or space of the dharmadhātu. *'Gro* means to go. Wisdom mind goes without obstruction in the sky of the dharmadhātu. The khadro performs the activities of the Buddha.

3. The Three Kāyas are the dharmakāya, sambhogakāya, and nirmāṇakāya.

Dharmakāya in Tibetan is *Chhos.sku. Chhos* means all phenomena. *sKu* means body. The true nature of all phenomena is without substance, shape, color, or form, not coming or going, not dwelling any place. It is without any reality; it is great emptiness. All phenomena are completely pervaded by or entirely contained within great emptiness: this is the emptiness-body or dharmakāya.

Sambhogakāya in Tibetan is *Longs.spyod.rdzogs.sku. Longs* means wealth, *spyod* means to use or enjoy, *rdzogs* means complete, *sku* means body. *Sambhogakāya* means the body of complete enjoyment of the wealth of pure perceptions.

Nirmāṇakāya in Tibetan is *sPrul.sku. sPrul* means to emanate or create. *sKu* means body. The unobstructed compassion of the buddhas is the basis of the nirmāṇakāya because the emanation bodies of nirmāṇakāya come from this unobstructed compassion.

According to the view of the vehicle of cause, concerning the Three Jewels, the only perfect refuge is the Buddha. The Dharma is the path which one follows to attain buddhahood. Once this state has been attained, the path is transcended,[1] just as the boat in which one crosses a river is left behind when the other shore is reached. The Saṅgha are the arhats and bodhisattvas, those who have not yet reached the state of buddhahood, so they are not considered omniscient. But one must not be

1. As mentioned in chapter 10 for the Dharmas of precept and realization.

careless, because while one is still on the path, one must rely upon the Dharma and the Saṅgha.

According to the view of the vehicle of result, the Buddha, Dharma, and Saṅgha are from the beginning the phenomena of full enlightenment. They are the inseparable manifestation of the three kāyas, filling the dharmadhātu. The immeasurable appearances of the Buddha, Dharma, and Saṅgha; the lama, yidam, and khadro; and the nirmāṇakāya, sambhogakāya, and dharmakāya are the inexhaustible, beginninglessly pure maṇḍala of Samantabhadra.

14

DHARMAKĀYA

DHARMAKĀYA (CHHOS.SKU) means the body of Dharma. All wisdom Dharmas are contained in the dharmakāya. There are twenty-one sets of outflowless[1] attributes of the dharmakāya, but the essence of all of these is great emptiness. According to the Dzogchen teachings, the quality of the dharmakāya is "possessing the two purities" (Dag.pa gnyis ldan), which are the "essence pure from the beginning" (Ngo.bo ye.nas dag.pa) and the purification of self-nature (Rang.bzhin.gyi rnam.par dag.pa). Sometimes the purification of self-nature is called purifying the momentary obscurations (gLo.bur.gyi dri.ma dag.pa).

The dharmakāya is great emptiness, but according to Mahāyāna,[2] dharmakāya also has the "qualities of the result of separation." These qualities are:

The *ten strengths* (Skt. dasha-bala; Tib. sTobs.bchu),
The *four fearlessnesses* (Skt. catur-vaiśāradya; Tib. Mi.'jigs.pa bzhi),
The *four analytical knowledges* (Skt. catuḥ-pratisaṃvid; Tib. So.so yang.dag pa'i rig.pa bzhi),

1. For example, karmically nonproductive.

2. According to Mahāyāna, the rūpakāya (gZugs.sku) which comprises both sambhogakāya and nirmāṇakāya (see chapters 15 and 16), has the "qualities of ripened result." These are the thirty-two noble marks (mTshan bzang.po sum.chu.rtsa.gnyis) and the eighty excellent signs (dPe byad brgyad.chu) of the Buddha. It is not possible to explain all these attributes here, but descriptions of them can be found in many texts.

The *three unguardednesses,* or ways of having nothing to hide (Skt. try-arakṣana; Tib. bSrung.ba med.pa rnam.pa gsum),

The *three nonpossessions* (Mi.mgna'.ba gsum),

The *four things pure in every aspect* (rNam.pa thams. chad dag.pa bzhi),

The *four knowledges of [others'] intent* (Skt. catuḥ-prāṇidhijñāna; Tib. sMon.gnas mkhyen.pa bzhi),

The *five eyes* (Skt. pañca-cakṣuḥ; Tib. sPyan lnga),

The *six supernatural perceptions* (Skt. ṣhaḍabhijñā; Tib. mNgon. shes drug),

The *ten powers* (Skt. dasha-vaṣitāḥ; Tib. dBang bchu),

The *three miracles* (Skt. tri-prātihārya; Tib. Chho.'phrul gsum),

The *six rememberings* (Skt. ṣaḍ-anusmṛti; Tib. rJes.dran drug),

The *eighteen unassociated qualities* (Ma.hdres.pa bcho. brgyad),[3] which are:

> The *six unassociated activities* (sPyod.pa ma.'dres.pa drug),
>
> The *six unassociated realizations* (rTogs.pa ma.'dres.pa drug),
>
> The *three unassociated words* (Phrin.las ma.'dres.pa gsum), and
>
> The *three wisdoms* (Ye.shes gsum).

3. Unassociated with any unenlightened qualities.

15

SAMBHOGAKĀYA

The Five Certainties

SAMBHOGAKĀYA (Longs.spyod rdzogs sku) means enjoying the wealth of the five certainties (Nges.pa lnga), which are certain place, certain teacher, certain retinue, certain time, and certain teaching.

1. According to the Mahāyāna, the five certainties are as follows:

The certain place is the Ogmin (Akaniṣṭha) buddhafield or universe within which are the buddhafields of the four directions and the center:

In the center is the buddhafield of Namparnangdzed (Vairocana), called Tugpoköpa;

In the east is the buddhafield of Mikyödpa (Akṣobhya), called Ngönpargawa;

In the south is the buddhafield of Rinchenjungne (Ratnasambhava), called Paldangdenpa;

In the west is the buddhafield of Nangwathaye (Amitābha), called Dewachen;

In the north is the buddhafield of Dönyöddrubpa (Amoghasiddhi), called Lerabdzogpa.

The certain teachers are the five victorious ones (jinas), the buddhas of these buddhafields. According to the general Mahāyāna system, they have the thirty-two noble marks (mTshan.bzang.po sum chu.rtsa.gnyis) and the eighty excellent signs (dPe.byad bzang.po brgyad.bchu).

The certain retinue in these buddhafields is not composed of ordinary individuals; it consists solely of tenth-stage bodhisattvas, such as Sayinyingpo (Kṣitigarbha), Chagnadorje (Vajrapāṇi), Namkhainyingpo (Skt. Ākāśagarbha), Chenrezig (Avlokiteśvara), Jampa (Maitreya), Dribpanamsel (Sarvanīvaraṇaviṣkambhin), Kuntuzangpo (Samantabhadra), Jampalyang (Mañjuśrī), etc.

The certain time is the perpetual, continuous teaching of the Dharma.

The certain Dharma teaching is the Mahāyāna doctrine.

The Ogmin (Skt. Akaniṣṭha) buddhafield of the Mahāyāna system is considered by the highest Vajrayāna to be a half-nirmāṇakāya, half-sambhogakāya buddhafield. (Phyed. sprul longs.sku) because in Ogmin the certain retinue or disciples are different from the certain teacher; that is, they are not his emanations. Since the disciples are tenth-stage bodhisattvas, they are nirmāṇakāya; since the teachers are the five buddhas, they are sambhogakāya.

2. According to the highest Vajrayāna, the five certainties are the following:

The certain place is the "Great Ogmin" ('Og.min Chhen.po) or Self-Nature Ogmin;

The certain teachers are the five buddhas with their consorts (Yab-yum);

The certain retinue are the fulfilled bodhisattvas, male and female, such as Sayinyingpo, Chagnadorje, Namkhainyingpo, Chenrezig, Gegmoma, Luma, Threngwama, Garma, etc;

The certain teachings are all the highest Vajrayāna teachings, and all sounds and words are characteristicless;

The certain time is the "timelessness of primordial purity" (Ka.dag.gi dus).

Since in the Ogmin Chenpo buddhafield of the highest Vajrayāna, the certain retinue are the fulfilled male and female bodhisattvas, they are the reflection of the five buddhas yab-yum (with consort), and their Wisdom Minds are not different from those of the five buddhas. Because of this, all the highest Vajrayāna teachings are displayed by the five buddhas to the fulfilled male and female bodhisattvas. Since the Wisdom Mind of the certain teacher and certain retinue is not different, and the certain teaching arises spontaneously, the question can be asked: why is there this teaching? It is a spontaneous gesture which is necessary for teaching the nirmāṇakāya. It is necessary because, without the dharmakāya, there is no sambhogakāya; without the sambhogakāya, there is no nirmāṇakāya; and without the nirmāṇakāya, there is no teaching for the benefit of sentient beings. But this spontaneous gesture is without motive, because the teaching is the natural manifestation of the Great Ogmin.

THE PEACEFUL SAMBHOGAKĀYA DEITIES
[Zhi.ba'i longs.spyod rdzogs.sku]

1. THE FIVE BUDDHA FAMILIES

The certain teachers in the Great Ogmin buddhafield of the Vajrayāna are the five jinas, or buddhas, with their consorts.

The "self-nature of the five skandhas, primordially pure, is the five buddhas" (Phung.po lnga ye.nas dag.pa'i rang.bzhin rgyal.ba rigs.lnga), and the "self-nature of the five passions, primordially pure, is the five wisdoms" (Nyon.mongs.pa lnga ye.nas dag.pa'i rang.bzhin ye.shes lnga):

The self-nature of the *skandha of form* (gZugs kyi

phung.po), primordially pure, is Namparnangdzed; and the self-nature of the passion of ignorance, primordially pure, is the *wisdom of the dharmadhātu* (Chhos.dbyings ye.shes);

The self-nature of the *skandha of consciousness* (rNams.shes kyi phung.po), primordially pure, is Mikyödpa; and the self-nature of the passion of anger or aversion, primordially pure, is the *mirror wisdom* (Me.long ye.shes);

The self-nature of the *skandha of feeling* (Tshor. ba'i phung.po), primordially pure, is Rinchenjungne; and the self-nature of the passion of pride, primordially pure, is the *all-equalizing wisdom* (mNyam.nyid ye.shes);

The self-nature of the *skandha of perception* ('Du.shes kyi phung.po), primordially pure, is Nangwathaye; and the self-nature of the passion of desire or attachment, primordially pure, is the *discriminating wisdom* (Sor.rtog ye.shes);

The self-nature of the *skandha of intention* ('Du.byed kyi phung.po), primordially pure, is Dönyöddrubpa; and the self-nature of the passion of jealousy, primordially pure, is the *all-accomplishing wisdom* (Bya.grub ye.shes).

The self-nature of the five elements, primordially pure, is the self-nature of the five consorts of the five buddhas:

The *self-nature of space,* primordially pure, is Yingkyi Wangchugma (Dhātvīśvarī);

The *self-nature of water,* primordially pure, is Māmakī;

The *self-nature of earth,* primordially pure, is Sanggyechenma (Buddha-locanā);

The *self-nature of fire,* primordially pure, is Gökarmo (Pāṇḍara-vāsinī);

The *self-nature of air,* primordially pure, is Damtshig Drölma (Samayatārā).

The body colors of the five buddhas are symbols of the predominant aspects which relate to the passions in the minds of individual sentient beings.[1]

The white body of Namparnangdzed is the symbol of being without any fault whatsoever;
The yellow body of Rinchenjungne is the symbol of possessing the greatest qualities;
The red body of Nangwathaye is the symbol of having the great love of aimless compassion for all sentient beings;
The green body of Dönyöddrubpa is the symbol of various activities;
The blue body of Mikyödpa is the symbol of the unchanging dharmatā.[2]

According to the highest Vajrayāna system, all the buddhas have the thirty-two noble marks and eighty excellent signs. They also emanate sixteen male bodhisattvas and sixteen female bodhisattvas, who together are also called the thirty-two noble marks. Each of the sixteen male bodhisattvas is adorned with the five crowns of the buddhas, all together making eighty crowns, which are also called the eighty excellent signs.

The thrones of the five buddhas of the maṇḍala are symbols of their qualities:

The snow-lion throne of the buddha in the center of the maṇḍala is the symbol that all five buddhas have the "four fearlessnesses" (Mi.'jigs.pa bzhi) which subdue the four demons;

1. Although each buddha may appear in his one body color symbolizing a predominant aspect, he possesses all of the qualities of all the buddhas, not just the one quality. A many-colored body is the symbol of containing all the qualities of the buddha families together.

2. According to different tantras, the body color and maṇḍala position of Namparnangdzed and Mikyödpa can be interchanged, so it is essential to understand each tantra system.

The elephant throne of the buddha in the east of the maṇḍala is the symbol that all five buddhas have the "ten strengths of wisdom" (sTobs bchu) which subdue the ten unvirtuous actions;

The supreme horse throne of the buddha in the south of the maṇḍala is the symbol that all five buddhas have the great attribute of the "four bases [lit. legs] of miraculous power" (rDzu.'phrul gyi rkang.pa bzhi), which enables unobstructed passage everywhere;

The peacock throne of the buddha in the west of the maṇḍala is the symbol that all five buddhas have the absolutely perfect "ten powers" (dBang bchu);

The garuḍa or "shang-shang" throne of the buddha in the north of the maṇḍala is the symbol that all five buddhas have the "four activities" (Phrin.las bzhi) which liberate one from birth and death;

> The many jewels of all the five thrones are symbols that all five buddhas are able to fulfill whatever needs sentient beings may have;
>
> The lotus which is on each throne is the symbol that all five buddhas remain in saṃsāra for the benefit of sentient beings but are unstained by its faults, like a flower which comes from the mud but is never touched by it;
>
> The sun and moon above each lotus are the symbols that all five buddhas have skillfull means and wisdom inseparably.

The articles held in the hands of the five buddhas, their retinues, and the wrathful deities are also symbolic:[3]

3. It is not possible to explain all of the many different articles here, but explanations of them can be found by a close examination of various tantric sādhanas. Only a few of the most general articles are explained here.

The Dharma Wheel is the symbol of cutting through the passions of saṃsāra;

The bell is the symbol of the sound of the dharmadhātu's great emptiness;

The dorje is the symbol of the indestructibility of all wisdom appearance of the dharmadhātu;

The precious jewel is the symbol of containing all good qualities;

The lotus is the symbol of constant, aimless compassion toward all sentient beings;

The sword is the symbol of cutting the net of existence;

The double dorje is the symbol of performing the various buddha activities; and

Weapons are the symbol of annihilating wrong views.

2. FULFILLED BODHISATTVAS

According to the highest Vajrayāna teachings, the certain retinue are the fulfilled male bodhisattvas and their consorts, the fulfilled female bodhisattvas, including:

The four inner male bodhisattvas: Sayinyingpo (Kṣitigarbha), Chagnadorje (Vajrapāṇi), Namkhainyingpo (Ākāśagarba), and Chenrezig (Avalokiteśvara);

Their consorts, the four inner female bodhisattvas: Gegmoma (Lāsyā), Luma (Gītā), Threngwama (Mālā), and Garma (Nṛtyā);

The four outer male bodhisattvas: Jampa (Maitreya), Dribpanamsel (Sarvanīvaraṇaviṣkambhin), Kuntuzangpo (Samantabhadra), and Jampalyang (Mañjuśrī);

Their consorts, the four outer female bodhisattvas: Dugpöma (Dhūpā), Metogma (Puṣōpā), Nangsalma (Ālokā), and Drichabma (Gaṅdhā);

The four male guardians: Shinjeshed (Yamāntaka), Tobpoche (Mahābala), Tamdrin (Hayagrīva), and Dudtsikhyilba (Amṛtakuṇḍalin);

Their consorts, the four female guardians: Chagkyuma (Aṅkuśā), Shagpama (Pāshā), Chagdrogma (Śṛnkhalā), and Drilbuma (Ghaṇṭā), and so on, all together with their retinues in their maṇḍalas.

The self-nature of the consciousness of the sense organs, primordially pure, is the four inner male bodhisattvas:

The self-nature of the consciousness of the eyes, primordially pure, is the bodhisattva Sayinyingpo;

The self-nature of the consciousness of the ears, primordially pure, is the bodhisattva Chagnadorje;

The self-nature of the consciousness of the nose, primordially pure, is the bodhisattva Namkhainyingpo;

The self-nature of the consciousness of the tongue, primordially pure, is the bodhisattva Chenrezig.

The self-nature of the sense organs, primordially pure, is the four outer male bodhisattvas:

The self-nature of the sense organ of the eyes, primordially pure, is the bodhisattva Jampa;

The self-nature of the sense organ of the ears, primordially pure, is the bodhisattva Dribpanamsel;

The self-nature of the sense organ of the nose, primordially pure, is the bodhisattva Kuntuzangpo;

The self-nature of the sense organ of the tongue, primordially pure, is the bodhisattva Jampalyang.

The self-nature of the objects of the sense organs, primordially pure, is the four inner female bodhisattvas:

The object of the eyes is form, and its self-nature, primordially pure, is the ḍākinī Gegmoma, whose name means charming or coquettish ḍākinī;

The object of the ears is sound, and its self-nature, primordially pure, is the ḍākinī Luma, whose name means singing ḍākinī;

The object of the nose is smell, and its self-nature, primordially pure, is the ḍākinī Threngwama, whose name means garland-wearing ḍākinī;

The object of the tongue is taste, and its self-nature, primordially pure, is the ḍākinī Garma, whose name means dancing ḍākinī.

The self-nature of thoughts or conceptions, primordially pure, is the four outer female bodhisattvas:

The self-nature of present conceptions or thoughts, primordially pure, is the ḍākinī Dugpöma, whose name means incense-offering ḍākinī;

The self-nature of previous conceptions or thoughts, primordially pure, is the ḍākinī Metogma, whose name means flower-offering ḍākinī;

The self-nature of future thoughts or conceptions, primordially pure, is the ḍākinī Nangselma, whose name means lamp-offering ḍākinī;

The self-nature of thoughts or conceptions of uncertain time, primordially pure, is the ḍākinī Drichabma, whose name means scented water–offering ḍākinī.

The self-nature of the body, primordially pure, is the four male guardians:

The self-nature of the consciousness of the body, primordially pure, is the guardian Shinjeshed;

The self-nature of the sense organs of the body, primordially pure, is the guardian Tobpoche;

The self-nature of the touch or feeling of the body, primordially pure, is the guardian Tamdrin;

The self-nature of the consciousness of the touch or feeling of the body, primordially pure, is the guardian Dudtsi-khyilba.

The self-nature of the four extreme points of view, primordially pure, is the four female guardians:

The self-nature of the eternalist point of view (rTag.par lta.ba), primordially pure, is the ḍākinī Chagkyuma, whose name means having-an-iron-hook ḍākinī;
The self-nature of the nihilist point of view (Chhad.par lta.ba), primordially pure, is the ḍākinī Shagpama, whose name means having-a-noose ḍākinī;
The self-nature of the point of view that there is ego (bDag.tu lta.ba), primordially pure, is the ḍākinī Chagdrogma, whose name means having-an-iron-chain ḍākinī;
The self-nature of the point of view that there is reality or substance (mTshan.mar lta.ba), primordially pure, is the ḍākinī Drilbuma, whose name means having-a-bell ḍākinī.

According to the highest Vajrayāna, the five buddhas and their five consorts, together with the sixteen male and female bodhisattvas and the eight male and female guardians, are the thirty-four peaceful deities in the sambhogakāya buddhafield of the self-nature pureland. According to certain sādhanas for practicing samādhi, these thirty-four peaceful sambhogakāya deities, Kuntuzangpo yab-yum, and the six buddha nirmāṇakāya emanations (see chapter 16) are the "forty-two peaceful deities in the samādhi maṇḍala" (Ting.nge 'dzin dkyil. 'khor).

3. THE NINE SIGNS OF THE WISDOM BODY (Zhi.ba'i tshul dgu)

There are nine signs of the wisdom body of the peaceful sambhogakāya deities:

A pliant body is the sign that ignorance has been purified;
A well-toned body is the sign that desire has been purified;
A delicate body is the sign that pride has been purified;
A perfectly proportioned body is the sign that anger or hatred has been purified;
A youthful appearance of the body is the sign that jealousy or envy has been purified;
A clear body is the sign that the defect of stains has been purified;
A radiant body is the sign of containing all excellent qualities;
An attractive body is the sign of having the perfection of all the thirty-two noble marks and eighty excellent signs together;
Splendor and blessing of the body are the signs of vanquishing all things.

4. THE THIRTEEN ADORNMENTS

The peaceful sambhogakāya deities wear the "thirteen adornments of the peaceful deities" (Tib. Zhi.ba'i rgyan.chhas bchu.gsum). These are the "five silken garments" (Tib. Dar gyi chhas gos lnga) and the "eight jewel ornaments" (Tib. Rin.po chhe'i rgyan.brgyad).

The five silken garments are:

Patterned blue silken scarf (Dar.mthing khra'i gzil ldir),
Five-colored crown pendants (Kha dog sna lnga'i chod.pan),
Upper garment of white silk with golden design (Dar dkar.po gser.gyi ngang.ris.chan.gyi stod.gyogs),
Lower skirt-like garment (Tshigs dgu'i smad dkris), and
Sleeves, as for dancing (Gar gyi phy.dung).

The eight jewel ornaments are:

Crown (dBurgyan),
Earrings (sNyan.rgyan),
Short throat necklace (mGul.rgyan),
Shoulder ornament (dPung.rgyan),
Middle necklace (Do.shal)
Long necklace (Se.mo.do),
Bracelets (Phyag.gdub), and
Anklets (Zhabs.gdub).[4]

THE WRATHFUL SAMBHOGAKĀYA DEITIES
[Long.spyod rdzogs.sku khro.bo]

The wrathful sambhogakāya deities are the "natural wisdom skill of the peaceful deities" (Zhi.ba'i rtsal) or "natural self-luminosity of the peaceful deities" (Zhi.ba'i rang.mdangs). Within peaceful, equanimitous wisdom, there is no demon of spiritual substantiality; there is no clinging to the duality of self and others. This is the "basic self-nature of the natural wrathful dharmatā" (Chhos.nyid ngang.gis khro.bo). There are many wrathful deities whose maṇḍalas are spontaneously self-created from the wisdom-skill of the five glorious herukas. These are the endless maṇḍalas of their own pure perceptions of body, speech, mind, excellent qualities and activities. Their wisdom body, wisdom speech, and wisdom mind have three aspects each, which are explained below as the "nine wrathful aspects." The number of excellent wisdom qualities is endless, and the two aspects of wisdom activities are the gestures of annihilating

4. According to some systems which omit the crown and anklets and include the "garland of flowers" (Me.tog.gi phreng.ba), there are seven jewel ornaments. These seven ornaments symbolize the "seven branches of enlightenment" (Byang.chhub kyi yan.lag bdun).

saṃsāra and guiding sentient beings to nirvāṇa. All together, these are the aspects of the wrathful sambhogakāya.

1. The five herukas are described as follows.

Chemchog Heruka is the lord, or principal heruka:

His dark-brown body color symbolizes that ignorance is not abandoned, but is spontaneously purified into the wisdom of the dharmadhātu;

His nine heads symbolize the nine states of being "joined in equanimity" (sNyoms.'jug dgu);

His eighteen arms symbolize the eighteen great emptinesses;

His eight legs symbolize the "eight deliverances" (Tib. rNam.thar brgyad; Skt. aṣṭau-vimokṣha);

His spread legs symbolize the wrathful aspect of subduing demons; and

Rudra, who is the cushion beneath his feet, symbolizes the annihilation of ordinary ego and the subduing by his wisdom skill of those beings like Rudra who come into the world.

Vajra Heruka's white body color is a symbol that anger or hatred is not abandoned, but is spontaneously purified into mirror wisdom.

Ratna Heruka's yellow body color is a symbol that pride is not abandoned, but is spontaneously purified into all-equalizing wisdom.

Padma Heruka's red body color is a symbol that desire is not abandoned, but is spontaneously purified into discerning wisdom.

Karma Heruka's green body color is a symbol that jealousy is not abandoned, but is spontaneously purified into all-accomplishing wisdom.

The three heads of each of these four herukas symbolize the three kāyas;

Their six arms symbolize annihilating the six kinds of consciousness which cause rebirth as the "six classes of beings" ('Gro.ba rigs drug);

Their four legs symbolize annihilating the "four kinds of saṃsāric birth" (sKye.gnas bzhi); and

The male and female rudra cushions under their feet symbolize subduing the "four demons" (bDud bzhi).

2. The nine wrathful aspects of the wrathful deities are the three of body, three of speech, and three of mind.

The three aspects of wisdom body are:

The wrathful deities show captivating aspects in order to lead beings who have desire out of saṃsāra;

They show heroic aspects in order to lead beings who have anger or hatred out of saṃsāra; and

They show fierce aspects in order to lead beings who have ignorance out of saṃsāra.

The three aspects of wisdom speech are:

They utter attracting, laughing sounds (like *ha, ha, hi, hi,* etc.) in order to lead beings who have desire out of saṃsāra;

They utter harsh, threatening sounds (like *huṃ, huṃ, phat, phat,* etc.) in order to lead beings who have anger or hatred out of saṃsāra; and

They utter wrathful, thunderous sounds (like *woor, woor, dir, dir,* etc.) in order to lead beings who have ignorance out of saṃsāra.

The three aspects of wisdom mind are as follows:

Their minds show compassion in order to lead beings who have desire out of saṃsāra;

Their minds show magnificent power in order to lead beings who have anger or hatred out of saṃsāra; and

Their minds show tranquillity in order to lead beings who have ignorance out of saṃsāra.

3. The eight graveyard adornments (Dur.khrod chhas brgyad) of the wrathful deities are described as follows:

The three garments (bGo.ba'i gos gsum), which are:

An elephant skin, which is a sign that ignorance has been subdued by the ten strengths;

A human skin, which is a sign that desire has been subdued by "desireless great compassion"; and

A tiger skin, which is a sign that anger or hatred has been subdued by "wrathful compassion."

The two kinds of fastened ornaments (gDags.pa'i rgyan gnyis), which are as follows:

Human skull ornaments, dried and fresh, which are:

The crown of five dry human skulls (Thod.pa skam.po lnga'i dbu.rgyan),

The garland of fifty fresh heads (rLon.pa lnga. bchu'i do.shal),

The bracelets of fragments of human heads (Tshal.bu'i dpung.rgyan), and

Snake ornaments, which are:

The white-spotted snake hair ribbon, which is an ornament that symbolizes subduing the caste of nāga kings;

The yellow-spotted snake earrings, which are an ornament that symbolizes subduing the caste of nāga nobility;

The red-spotted snake necklace, which is an ornament that symbolizes subduing the Brahmin caste of nāgas;

The green-spotted snake bracelets, which are an ornament that symbolizes subduing the ordinary caste of nāgas; and

The black-spotted snake belt or sash, which is an ornament that symbolizes subduing the lowest caste of nāgas.

The three smeared things (Byug.pa'i rdzas gsum) symbolizing the subduing of jealousy, which are:

Ashes piled on the forehead,
Blood spotting the bridge of the nose or cheeks, and
Moldy grease smeared on the chin.

These eight graveyard adornments together with the blazing fire of wisdom (Ye.shes kyi me.dpung) and the vajra wings (rDo.rje'i gshog.pa) are the ten glorious adornments (dPal.gyi chhas bchu).

According to another system, the eight glorious adornments are explained as follows.

The crocodile skin is symbolic of shining with splendor;
The sun and moon symbolize skillful means and wisdom inseparable;
The fire of wisdom symbolizes burning noxious beings;
The crescent-moon-shaped fangs or canine teeth symbolize cutting through birth and death;
The vajra garments symbolize being completely mighty;
The armor of power symbolizes dwelling in the state of buddhahood; and
The iron double vajra symbolizes reversing harm.

4. The male deities have six bone ornaments:

A hair net of bone pendants hanging from the uṣṇīṣa,[5]
Bone earrings,
A short bone necklace,
A long bone necklace,

5. Crest on top of the head.

A bone girdle, and
Bone bracelets and anklets.

5. The female deities have the five mudrā ornaments symbolizing the five wisdoms:

The wisdom of the dharmadhātu is shown by the cakra on the crown of the head;
Discerning wisdom is shown by the pair of earrings;
All-equalizing wisdom is shown by the short necklace;
Mirror wisdom is shown by the bracelets and anklets;
All-accomplishing wisdom is shown by the girdle.

There is also another system which explains the six bone mudrā ornaments for female deities:

Bone jewels on the right and left lower shoulders,
Bone lotuses on the breast,
Bone vajras on the back,
Bone cakras on the right and left shoulder blades,
A bone eternal knot at the waist, and
A bone double vajra at the navel.

There are also various adornments and symbolic objects held in the hands of peaceful and wrathful deities. However, because there are so many different kinds of deities according to different sādhanas, each with many different symbolic objects, it is not possible to list them all here. They can be found by examining each sādhana.

All of the outer Ogmin Chenpo maṇḍala in which the peaceful and wrathful sambhogakāya deities dwell comes from the skill of these deities, and all is pure buddhafield; nothing is soiled or impure.

THE SEVEN BRANCHES OF CONJUNCTION

According to the highest Vajrayāna system, the sambhogakāya has the seven branches of conjunction (Kha.sbyor yan.lag bdun). Since the three kāyas are different aspects of the same essence, all the qualities of the dharmakāya and nirmāṇakāya are contained within the sambhogakāya. The seven branches of conjunction of the sambhogakāya comprise the three branches of nirmāṇakāya, the three branches of sambhogakāya, and the one branch of dharmakāya together.

The three qualities of the seven branches of conjunction which refer to the nirmāṇakāya are "great aimless compassion," "continuity," and "ceaselessness." Nirmāṇakāya is:

> Filled with great aimless compassion (dMigs.med snying.rje chhen.po);
>
> Through this compassion, "continuously, and without interruption" (rGyun mi.'chhad) entering into activity in the realms of sentient beings; and
>
> Always "effortlessly and ceaselessly" ('Gog.pa med.pa) doing whatever activity is of benefit to sentient beings.

The three qualities of the seven branches which refer to the sambhogakāya are "inseparably joined," "great bliss," and "complete enjoyment." According to this description, the sambhogakāya is:

> "Inseparably joined" (Kha.sbyor) with the "goddesses of wisdom's self-luminosity" (Ye.shes rang 'od kyi lha.mo rnams);
>
> Through this joining, completely filled with the "great bliss which is free from karmic outflows" (Zag.pa med.pa'i bde.ba chhen.po); and
>
> Of the essence of the five certainties and "always sustaining the Dharma of the wisdom lineage" (dGongs.brgyud kyi chhos), and hence "in perfect enjoyment of wealth possessions" (Longs.spyod rdzogs.pa).

The quality of the seven branches of conjunctiòn which refers to the dharmakāya is "without self-nature." This means:

> Even though having these excellent qualities of aspects, the insubstantial or desireless essence is "without self-nature" (Rang.bzhin med.pa).

16

NIRMĀṆAKĀYA

NIRMĀṆAKĀYA (SPRUL.SKU) means emanation body. There are three or four different kinds of sPrul.sku, or tulku, emanations:

- Artisan emanations (bZo.yi sprul.sku), which are art such as thangka paintings, sculpture, etc., and artists who make them for the benefit of sentient beings;
- Birth emanations (sKye.ba'i sprul.sku) who take birth in forms such as monks, officials, hunters, prostitutes, blacksmiths, animals, etc., in order to benefit sentient beings;
- "Various things" emanations (sNa.tshogs kyi sprul.sku), which are images, mountains, rocks, valleys, pleasant houses, bridges, gardens, jewels, horses, food, clothes, etc., emanated in order to benefit sentient beings;[1] and
- Supreme emanations (mChhog.kyi sprul.sku), which are all those who fulfill the twelve deeds which all buddhas perform, as the Buddha Śākyamuni did.[2]

The Nirmāṇakāya or emanation buddhafields are such places as Shambhala, Changlochen, Zangdogpalri, etc.

According to the Nyingmapa tantric teachings, there are six mighty emanations of the Buddha who are the lords of the six

1. Sometimes the "various things" emanations are included among birth emanations.
2. See chapter 1.

realms of rebirth. In each realm, they emanate in the same form as the beings of that realm to benefit them. The self-natures of the six realms and the six passions, primordially pure, are these six emanations of the Nirmāṇakāya Buddha in the six realms:

The self-nature of the gods' realm and of pride, primordially pure, is the buddha Gyajin (Indra), lord of gods;

The self-nature of the asuras' or jealous gods' realm and of jealousy, primordially pure, is the buddha Thagzangri (Vemacitra), lord of the asuras;

The self-nature of the human realm and of desire, primordially pure, is the Buddha Sakyathubpa or Śākyamuni, lord of humans;

The self-nature of the animal realm and of ignorance, primordially pure, is the buddha Sengge Rabten, lord of the animals;

The self-nature of the yidag or hungry ghost realm and of greed, primordially pure, is the buddha Khabar (Jvālamukha), lord of the yidags; and

The self-nature of the hell realm and of anger or hatred, primordially pure, is the buddha Chökyigyalpo (Dharmarāja), lord of hell.[3]

THE FIVE UNCERTAINTIES

All of the qualities of the Nirmāṇakāya can be contained in the "five uncertainties" (Ma.nges.pa lnga), which are uncertain place, uncertain teacher, uncertain retinue, uncertain time, and uncertain teaching.

The uncertain place is among the six realms of beings;

The uncertain time is whenever the time to guide the minds of disciples (sentient beings) arises;

3. Each buddha purifies not only one realm and passion, but all purify all the realms and all the passions.

The uncertain teacher is whatever various forms may be appropriate for guidance;

The uncertain retinue are the three kinds of beings (followers of Hīnayāna, Mahāyāna, Vajrayāna) to be guided; and

The uncertain Dharma teachings are the various Hīnayāna, Mahāyāna, and Vajrayāna doctrines, etc.

There are both peaceful (Zhi.ba) and wrathful (Khro.bo) deities because, from the beginning, all sentient beings have the very nature of the peaceful or wrathful dharmatā, but through ignorance they do not recognize this nature. From this ignorance, duality arises; from duality, desire for object arises, and with this desire comes bliss. For this reason, the peaceful form of the compassionate unobstructed Nirmāṇakāya Buddha arises spontaneously, and the blissful blessing of the deity is an antidote for desire. From duality, hatred for undesired objects also arises, and with this hatred comes pride and cruelty which harms oneself and other sentient beings. For this reason, the wrathful form of the compassionate ceaseless Nirmāṇakāya Buddha spontaneously arises, and when one sees this form, cruelty and hatred are annihilated and sentient beings are held on the path to nirvāṇa.

Even though all sentient beings have different temperaments, moods, and senses, all these can be contained in the peaceful and wrathful aspects. In the same way, there are many different kinds of deities who can also be contained within the categories of peaceful and wrathful deities.

The compassionate wrathful nirmāṇakāya deities are those who subdue and guide on the path to nirvāṇa beings whose minds are without peace and who have harmful thoughts toward all other sentient beings, wishing to hinder their temporary happiness and their ultimate attainment of nirvāṇa.

According to the text of *The Gathering of Wisdom Mind* (dGongs 'dus), the compassionate wrathful Nirmāṇakāya deities came into this world in the following way. Many kalpas ago, in the Kalpa Kunöd (Sarvaprabha), the teaching of Mikyödpa (Akṣobhya) Buddha came to the land of Ngönpargawa (Abhirati) and the monk Thubkashönnu taught many Vajrayāna teachings. The landlord Keukaya lived near him, and Keukaya's son, Tharpanagpo, and servant, Denphag, went together to Thubkashönnu to receive tantric teachings. They asked Thubkashönnu if it was possible to practice Dharma without abandoning the passions, and he answered, "Yes, it is possible." Then he taught them: "If one's natural mind is uncontrived, then even if one steals, commits adultery, or lies, it does not matter. However many clouds fill the sky, the sky remains without fault. This is the path of the highest tantra [yoga]."

Having received this teaching, they returned and practiced separately. Although Tharpanagpo did not realize the meaning of the teaching and did not recognize the nature of his mind, he practiced killing, stealing, adultery, and lying, only grasping at the high terms of the teaching and misusing them. Denphag realized the meaning of the teachings and recognized the nature of his mind.

Tharpanagpo's and Denphag's points of view and activities did not agree and they debated, so they went to their teacher to ask him who was correct. When Thubkashönnu said that Denphag was correct, Tharpanagpo became very angry, abused and exiled both Thubkashönnu and Denphag, and continued to practice killing, stealing, adultery, and lying. He lived with the most terrible wild animals in graveyards and wore their skins as garments. He committed adultery with all females he saw; he killed all males he saw, drank their blood, ate their flesh, and wore their skins as a garment and their heads as an ornament.

When he died, Tharpanagpo was reborn in the lower realms

and had to endure very great misery as a result of his misuse of tantra. When he was reborn again in the human realm, he was not born as a normal human but in the form of Rudra, a terrible, wrathful demon. Because of his previous bad habits, he killed many beings including tigers, elephants, and humans, and he wore a tiger-skin skirt, cloaks of elephant skin and human skin, a crown of human skulls on his head, and a necklace of human heads as ornaments.

Glorious Heruka subdued Rudra and took all his skins and ornaments to wear himself as a sign of bravery. Rudra offered his body, and it became the cushion under glorious Heruka's feet. Then glorious Heruka bestowed his wisdom blessing on Rudra's mind and held it inseparable from his own wisdom mind. All Rudra's retinue were subdued and transformed into the maṇḍala of deities. They went before glorious Heruka and, offering their bodies, speech, and minds to him, they beseeched him to guide them on the path to liberation. They said to him, "If we cannot be lords ourselves, then we must become your retinue, and we will protect whoever makes prayers to your maṇḍala. If we are not fortunate enough to eat your first fruit offerings, please allow us to eat whatever is put outside when you have finished." For this reason the "leftovers" (Tshogs. lhag) are left outside when making "collections of offerings" (Tshogs).

In another explanation of this history, from the Ogmin Pureland, the Buddha ordered Vajrapāṇi to subdue Rudra. When he was subdued, Rudra offered his body to Vajrapāṇi as a cushion for his feet, and he was reborn as the Tathāgata Thalwei Wangpo.[4]

4. There are a number of other explanations for the subduing of Rudra.

17

CARRYING THE SIX GATHERINGS ON THE PATH

WHEN SITTING IN FORMAL meditation, we should practice nyam shag meditation.[1] When we arise from this meditation and are going, staying, eating, and speaking to others, when unhappiness or happiness arises, we should practice "carrying the six gatherings on the path."[2]

The senses (dBang.po) arise from consciousness (rNam. shes), and through these senses we perceive an object (Yul). However, this object also arises from consciousness, which is the subject. A gathering (Tshogs) is the conjunction of the object, the senses, and consciousness. Feelings such as hatred, anger, desire, pride, jealousy, etc., are all passions. They arise when we perceive objects, and through these passions we make karma.

For example, when a man sees a beautiful woman and falls in love with her, the woman is the object, and the senses and consciousness which perceive the woman are the subject. If the man did not have senses, he could not perceive the woman.

---

1. See footnote 5 on page 98.
2. Tshogs drug lam khyer. *Tshogs*: gathering; *drug*: six; *lam*: path; *khyer*: carry.

Without eyes he could not see form. But even with eyes, if he had no consciousness, he still could not perceive an object. In order to perceive, all three are needed together: object, senses, and consciousness; and the conjunction of these three is called a gathering.

When a man perceives a beautiful woman and desire arises in him, he wants to make love with her. But if this woman does not like him, or if she likes him but another man loves her, then anger arises in him. If this woman decides to go with another man, then jealousy arises. If he thinks that he must defeat this other man, win this woman for himself, and control her, then pride arises. If he is able to win this woman for himself and is staying with her, then anxiety constantly arises through his fear that he will lose her, and this is greed. All these five passions arise from ignorance, which is the basis of all passions. These five passions together with ignorance make the "six passions."[3] This example is also true for women who perceive beautiful men, for all these passions arise in the same way.

Depending on desire, anger arises; depending on anger, jealousy arises; depending on jealousy, pride arises; depending on pride, greed arises; and all these passions arise out of and are pervaded by ignorance.

Because of these passions, we make many habits. The way in which habits are formed can be explained by continuing with the example of the beautiful woman. All day long the six passions arise in the man because he is involved with the woman as the object of his passions. In all that he does, says, and thinks about her, desire, jealousy, and the other passions arise. Then at night he dreams of her and he dreams that he loves her, that

3. When all the passions are included in the "five passions," then greed has been included with desire. When they are all contained in the "three passions," pride has been included with anger or hatred, and jealousy has been included with desire.

he is angry or jealous, and so on; and thus his habits are formed. All the actions, speech, and thoughts of the six passions in which he engages in the day come to him in his dreams at night, forming his habits. These habits become stronger and stronger and are carried over from day to day, year to year, and from lifetime to lifetime. All experience or karma arises from these habits, and these habits come from the six passions.

An opposite example of arising passions is the example of a person who sees his enemy. At first, the sight of his enemy causes hatred to arise. From this hatred comes the thought that he must defeat this enemy and become victorious, which is pride. From this pride comes the hope or desire to have success. From desire comes the greed of wishing to hold always to this success. From this greed comes the jealousy of thinking that another will become greater than he is. All these five passions arise out of ignorance, as in the previous example.

These passions arise in the same way through all the senses: through hearing unpleasant or pleasant sounds, blame or praise; through smelling bad or good odors; through tasting unsavory or delicious flavors; through touching rough or soft surfaces; through seeing ugly or beautiful forms; and through experiencing unhappy or happy feelings. The sixth sense is the sense of consciousness; although each of the other senses perceives differently, the sense of consciousness which knows functions in all of them. Consciousness is like a monkey in a house with five windows which are like the five senses. When the monkey leaps around inside the house, moving quickly from window to window, it may seem as if there are many monkeys inside the house, but in fact there is only one monkey.

The conjunction of the object, the sense organ, and the consciousness of each of the six senses is called the six gatherings of consciousness (rNam.shes tshogs drug). All human beings have the six gatherings of consciousness. Saṃsāra arises from these gatherings, and all human beings wander in saṃsāra because of them.

How do we carry these six gatherings on the path to liberation?

To continue with the example of the beautiful woman, when desire arises upon seeing a beautiful woman, if the man is practicing this meditation, he should not repress this desire, but should just let it go and watch to see what the essence of the desire is. There is no substance or root of this desire; there is no place where this desire dwells, so this desire automatically vanishes. When this desire vanishes, the object of desire automatically vanishes with it. Since there is no desire, anger does not arise. In the same way, there is no jealousy, pride, or greed because the object of these passions has vanished. The object of these passions has dissolved into the subject, or consciousness, and consciousness dissolves into the dharmadhātu. Since there are no longer any of the five passions, ignorance has vanished, and this is liberation.

When any of the six gatherings arise from our sense of hearing, smelling, tasting, etc., we should not repress them, but should use them in our meditation. In the same way that desire or hatred vanish by this practice of carrying the six gatherings on the path, so also jealousy, pride, and greed will vanish. Whenever a passion arises from perceiving an object of that passion, if we practice, this passion will vanish and the object of the passion will vanish along with it. This is the practice of "carrying the six gatherings on the path to liberation." If one can practice this method, then the more the passions arise, the greater the benefit will be. Because our minds are always mixed with the passions, when the passions arise strongly we can have a greater understanding of the condition of our minds. However, if we cannot practice this method, when the passions arise strongly we will just be making strong karma.

Liberation means freedom from the ties of saṃsāra. These ties are the passions which bind us and cause us to wander endlessly in saṃsāra. Freedom comes from the practice of using the passions and freeing ourselves from the karma of these passions. This is the self-liberation of the six gatherings (Tshogs drugs rang.grol).[4]

When we sit to practice meditation, we should meditate on leaving the mind in equanimity (mNyam.bzhag),[5] and we should practice freedom from the five skandhas (Phung.po lnga dang bral.ba).[6] When we leave our formal meditation and carry on the daily activities of eating, sleeping, walking, etc., we should practice "carrying the six gatherings on the path to liberation."

4. Tshogs drug rang.grol. *Tshogs*: gathering; *drug*: six; *rang*: self; *grol*: liberation.

5. mNyam.bzhag. *mNyam*: equanimity; *bzhag*: to leave.

6. Phung.po lnga dang bral.ba. *Phung.po*: skandha; *lnga*: five; *dang bral.ba*: free from. See chapter 19.

18

THE STAGES OF DISSOLVING

THE FIVE INNER ELEMENTS OF flesh, blood, body heat, space, and consciousness are dependent on the five outer elements of earth, water, fire, wind, and sky. At the time of death, the five inner elements gradually dissolve into one another. In order not to be afraid at this time, we should know what the "stages of dissolving" (Thim.rim)[1] are so that we will recognize them.

The earth element, which corresponds to the flesh of the body, dissolves into water. At this time the body becomes very heavy and we feel as though we cannot move.

The water element, which corresponds to the blood of the body, dissolves into fire or heat. At this time we feel very dry because the water in the body is evaporating. Some people, not recognizing the stages of dissolving, will ask for water and drink as much as they can, believing that it will stop the feeling of dryness.

The fire element, which corresponds to body heat, dissolves into air or breath. At this time the heat leaves the body and we feel cold.

The wind or air element, which corresponds to space, dis-

1. Thim.rim. *Thim*: dissolve; *rim*: order.

solves into consciousness. At this time we can no longer inhale or exhale; we can no longer breathe.

When all the elements have dissolved into consciousness, we feel as if we are being crushed under a great mountain.

When consciousness is in the body, the body is the support of consciousness; but when we die, because our consciousness has completely separated from our body, there is no longer any feeling of weight connected to consciousness. Because of this, we have the experience of falling. Since the power of all of the five sense organs is completely gone, we lose our phenomenal perception and fall into a state of unconsciousness. Everything becomes dark. Although each bardo, or in-between state, has a particular experience of perception, at this point we are not in any bardo at all, and because of the absence of sense organs, there are no perceptions except for the perception of darkness.

At the time when consciousness dissolves into space, which is like fainting, if we have had a good realization of the great emptiness of the dharmakāya while meditating in our previous life and have confidence in this understanding, then we will recognize this state and will be liberated in the dharmakāya. If we do not recognize this state, then after this, the sounds and forms of many peaceful and wrathful sambhogakāya deities appear to our perception. If in our previous life we have had good practice in visualizing our yidam, and have confidence in this visualization, then according to our own perception we will recognize the deities and will be liberated in the sambhogakāya. If we are afraid, and are not liberated by these deities appearing to our perception, but we remember to pray to go to a pure buddhafield, such as Zangdog Palri or Dewachen, then we will be liberated in the tulku, the nirmāṇakāya.

19

OṂ MA ṆI PAD ME HŪṂ

AN EXPLANATION OF THE SIX-syllable mantra, OṂ MA ṆI PAD ME HŪṂ, follows.

OṂ closes the door to the suffering of being reborn in the gods' realm. The suffering of the gods arises from foreseeing one's fall from the gods' realm. This suffering comes from pride.

MA closes the door to the suffering of being reborn in the warring gods' (asuras') realm. The suffering of these asuras is constant fighting. This suffering comes from jealousy.

ṆI closes the door to the suffering of being reborn in the human realm. The suffering of humans is birth, sickness, old age, and death. This suffering comes from desire.

PAD[1] closes the door to the suffering of being reborn in the animal realm. The suffering of animals is stupidity, preying upon one another, being killed by men for meat, skins, etc., and being beasts of burden. This suffering comes from ignorance.

ME closes the door to the suffering of being reborn in the hungry ghosts' realm. The suffering of hungry ghosts is hunger and thirst. This suffering comes from greed.

HŪṂ[2] closes the door to the suffering of being reborn in the hell realm. The suffering of the hells is heat and cold. This suffering comes from anger or hatred.

OṂ MA ṆI PAD ME HŪṂ

1. Pronounced *pay*.
2. Pronounced *hung*.

20

NGÖNDRO MEDITATION PRACTICE

Before we begin our daily meditation, we should clean our room and prepare our altar by cleaning it and making offerings. If we have no altar, we do not need to worry, we can simply visualize Padmasambhava in front of us.

The seven offering bowls which are offered on the altar symbolize the seven offerings:

> Water for drinking,
> Water for washing hands and feet,
> Flowers for adorning the head or hair,
> Incense for smelling to please the nose,
> Lamp for seeing to please the eyes,
> Perfumed water to sprinkle on the body, to refresh it, and
> Food to please the taste.

Music to please the ears can be an eighth offering.

The offerings which we make on the altar are symbolic. In our minds we offer all pleasant things that we see, hear, taste, smell, and feel. We offer the light of the sun and the moon, all fresh flowers, all pleasing smells, all delicious food, and so forth, everything wonderful. Since these offerings are made to the Three Jewels and the Three Roots, who do not have any greed or desire for these offerings, they are made for the benefit of all sentient beings.

After we have prepared our room and our altar, we begin our meditation with the common outer practice which is the four thoughts to turn the mind. These are:

The preciousness of human birth,
Impermanence and death,
The cause and effect of karma, and
The suffering of saṃsāra.

By meditating on these four thoughts, the mind is subdued and one is led to renounce saṃsāra.

Then we do the extraordinary inner preparation, which is the preliminary practice (sNgon.'gro). Within the Ngöndro, there is going for refuge, generating bodhicitta, Vajrasattva purification, maṇḍala offering, and the prayer of Guru Yoga (bLa.ma'i rnal.'byor).

Going for Refuge. Remembering and thinking about their qualities, we go for refuge in the Three Jewels. Paṇḍita Vimalamitra explained the motivation of going for refuge: "Remembering the suffering of saṃsāra and the qualities of nirvāṇa, we go for refuge until enlightenment is reached."

Generating Bodhicitta. Bodhicitta arises as we work for the attainment of enlightenment for the benefit of all other sentient beings.

Vajrasattva Purification. Whatever sins and obscurations we have made from beginningless time until now are purified by repenting to Vajrasattva using the "four powers."

Maṇḍala Offering. When making maṇḍala offerings, it is important not to think one-sidedly of offering to just one buddhafield, but to offer to all the buddhafields of all the three kāyas of all the buddhas of the ten directions. We should also not think one-sidedly of offering just one kind of thing, but should offer all kinds of wonderful things, substantial and insubstantial, created by mind, and we should not think one-sidedly of offering only for our own benefit, but should offer for the benefit of all sentient beings as extensive as the sky.

Guru Yoga. There are many kinds of visualization which are used for Guru Yoga. One is called "visualizing like gathering in the market." In this, the root lama (rTsa.ba'i bla.ma) is surrounded by many lamas of the lineage, yidams, ḍākas and ḍākinīs, buddhas, Dharma, and Saṅgha. Another is called "visualized in tiers." In this, the lamas sit one above the head of another. Another is called the "system of gathering all together into the jewel." In this, only the jewel-like vajra master is visualized. This means that the essence of all buddhas is gathered together into the varja master. We may practice whichever method we find convenient. In order to obtain the blessing of wisdom, we visualize ourselves as the wisdom ḍākinī. It is not that the varja master has desire for women, but rather that the wisdom ḍākinī is without obscuration, and by visualizing ourselves in this pure form, we can quickly obtain the blessing of wisdom.

When we have visualized the lama in front and ourselves as the wisdom ḍākinī, we recite the seven-branch prayer for accumulating merit:

> We prostrate as an antidote for pride. We emanate hundreds, thousands, millions, countless numbers of body emanations to make prostrations before the lama. Making prostrations purifies obscurations, brings benefit to our body in the present and all future lives, and helps us to attain the body of wisdom and many other excellent qualities.
>
> We offer as an antidote for greed. We offer all our various substantial possessions, as well as offerings emanated by mind, enough to fill the sky. The benefit of these

offerings is that great merit is made and fortunate opportunities come to us.

We confess as an antidote for anger or hatred. We confess and make strong repentance for breaking Hīnayāna, Mahāyāna, and Vajrayāna vows. The benefit of this confession is that we are liberated from the suffering of the lower three realms.

We rejoice as an antidote for jealousy. We rejoice in all virtues, with and without karmic outflows, because in so doing, we share in the virtues made by others.

We request as an antidote for ignorance. We request the buddhas and bodhisattvas not to remain quiet, but to turn the Wheel of Dharma and to teach the Dharma for the benefit of all sentient beings. The benefit of this request to turn the Wheel of Dharma is that in this and future lives we will be able to hear the teachings of the precious Dharma.

We pray as an antidote for disbelief. We pray to the buddhas not to depart into nirvāṇa, but to remain amid saṃsāra's suffering in order to help sentient beings. The benefit of this prayer for the buddhas to remain is that the sins we have committed in harming the lives of sentient beings are purified.

We dedicate as an antidote for doubt. We dedicate all the merit that has been gained so that we and all sentient beings may reach the state of enlightenment. The benefit is that all the virtue that we accumulate will not be exhausted until the time we reach enlightenment.

After we finish the seven-branch prayer, we recite the mantra

OṂ AḤ HŪṂ VAJRA GURU PADMA SIDDHI HŪṂ

one hundred times, one thousand times, or as many times as we can at one sitting. The meaning of this mantra is as follows.

OṂ is the essence syllable of the wisdom body of all the buddhas.

AḤ is the essence syllable of the wisdom speech of all the buddhas.

HŪṂ[1] is the essence syllable of the wisdom mind of all the Buddhas.[2]

VAJRA (rDo.rje) means indestructible, never divisible, never holding to the phenomena of duality. The dorje has seven dharma characteristics: it is uncuttable, indestructible, true, firm, fixed, completely unobstructed, and completely undefeatable. In this system, the name given to the dharmakāya is Nangwathaye or Öpame.[3]

GURU means lama. *La* means "life itself," that which is so precious; *ma* means "mother," because just as a mother has great love for her children, so the great aimless compassion of the dharmakāya arises spontaneously in the sambhogakāya form of Thugjechenpo[4] (Chenrezig). Lama also means *lanamepa* or unsurpassable because there is no one more precious than the lama. The lama always dwells within the sambhogakāya's seven branches of conjunction.[5]

PADMA[6] means lotus. Just as the lotus grows from the mud but the mud never stains the lotus, Padmasambhava always remains in saṃsāra to benefit sentient beings, but he is never obscured by the faults of saṃsāra. Also, if all buddhas are collected into the five buddha families, then Padmasambhava is

1. Pronounced *hung*.

2. These are the three introductory mantras.

3. Nangwathaye. *Nangwa*: pure perception; *thaye:* endless. All perceptions of the dharmakāya are pure; they are endless pure perception.

4. *Thugje* means "compassion"; *chenpo* means "great."

5. Explained in chapter 15 as great aimless compassion, continuity, ceaselessness, inseparably joined, great bliss which is free from karmic outflow, complete enjoyment, and without self-nature.

6. Pronounced *pay-ma*.

in the padma or lotus family, because he is the nirmāṇakāya emanation of the dharmakāya Nangwathaye and sambhogakāya Thugjechenpo, who are the padma or lotus family.

SIDDHI (dNgos.grub) refers to attainment of "general siddhi" (Thun.mong gi dngos.grub) and "supreme siddhi" (mChhog gi dngos.grub).

There are four general or common siddhi:

Peaceful (Zhi.ba): pacifying and purifying obscurations by peaceful activities;

Increasing (rGyas.pa): life, merit, intellect, and so on, increase by increasing activity;

Powerful (dBang): all phenomena are brought under our power by powerful activity;

Wrathful (Drag.po): all evil forces are subdued out of compassion by wrathful activities.

The supreme siddhi contains the five buddha families, the five buddha bodies, or kāyas, and the five wisdoms.

The five buddha families are the

Tathāgata family of body,
Lotus family of speech,
Vajra family of wisdom,
Jewel family of qualities, and
Amoghasiddhi family of activity.

The five buddha bodies, or kāyas, are the

Dharmakāya,
Sambhogakāya,
Nirmāṇakāya,
Body of "manifest enlightenment" (Tib. mNgon.par byang.chhub; Skt. Abhisambodhi), which is the various unmixed perceptions of the above three kāyas, and

"Essence body" (Tib. Ngo.bo nyid.sku; Skt. Svabhāvika-kāya), the essence of the four kāyas, which is always one.

The five wisdoms are the

Wisdom of dharmadhātu,
Mirror wisdom,
All-equalizing wisdom,
Discerning wisdom, and
All-accomplishing wisdom.

HŪṂ means "Please bestow upon me the blessings of the general and supreme siddhi."[7]

After reciting the mantra, we receive the four empowerments by the light which streams from Padmasambhava. Then the lama Padmasambhava dissolves into us and we remain in nyam shag meditation (samādhi).

The essential characteristic of nyam shag meditation is that it is free from the five skandhas. The essential characteristics of the five skandhas are:

Destructibility or breakability is the essential characteristic of the skandha of form;

Experiencing or desire is the essential characteristic of the skandha of feeling;

Movement or following after object is the essential characteristic of the skandha of perception;

Performing activities and gathering propensities is the essential characteristic of the skandha of intention;

Perception and creation of object is the essential characteristic of the skandha of consciousness.

7. This is one simple explanation of this mantra. Although it has many meanings and explanations, this is the only one which will be given now.

Nyam shag meditation is free from the five skandhas because

It does not have color or shape, so it is separate from the skandha of form;

It is "not attached to experiences" (Myong rig),[8] so it is separate from the skandha of feeling;

It is "without intention or aim to separate or discriminate" (Tha dad), so it is separate from the skandha of perception;

It is "without motivation" (Kun slong), so it is separate from the skandha of intention;

There is no holding or grasping to object or phenomena, so it is separate from the skandha of consciousness.

The four essential characteristics of nyam shag meditation, which is meditating in calm abiding (shi.ne) and sublime seeing (lhag.tong) inseparably, are that it is luminous, clear, radiant, and without conception. It is very difficult for beginning meditators to actually meditate shi.ne and lhag.tong inseparably as the "sublime" (Tib. 'Phags.pa) meditators do, but we must still try.

When arising from nyam shag meditation, we should pray for the lama's long life, and, finally, we should dedicate all the merit which has been gained for the benefit of all sentient beings, that they may quickly attain enlightenment.

8. Literally, "taste-knowing."

INDEX

Abhidharma. *See* Tripitaka
absolute truth, 4, 5, 31–33, 36–37, 40–46
actual relative truth. *See* relative truth
air, 34, 61–62; *see also* rLung
Amoghasiddhi family. *See* Buddha families
anger, 47, 55, 73, 79, 81–84, 90, 94–98, 101, 105
Anuyoga. *See* Doctrine of Result
Arhat, 28, 66
Atīśa, 17, 20, 23
Atiyoga. *See* Doctrine of Result
Avalokiteśvara (Chenrezig, sPyan.ras.gzigs), 4, 9, 51, 71, 76, 77, 106–107
awareness, 39

Ba.rdo, 33, 100
being, 30
Berwapa, 18
birth, 103
bliss, 30, 33, 34, 39, 62, 87, 91
Bodhgayā, 4
bodhicitta, 24, 26, 53, 61, 103
bodhisattvas, 4, 5, 30–31, 42–43, 48, 66, 74, 105
  fulfilled bodhisattvas, 9, 70–72, 76–80
  tenth stage bodhisattvas, 9, 54, 70–72
Bodhisattvayāna. *See* Doctrine of Cause
Bodongpa. *See* Tibetan Buddhism
Bönpo, 14
Buddha, 1, 3–5, 9–10, 17, 23, 40, 43–46, 50–54, 64–67, 89–90, 93
  disciples of, 4–6
  refuge in, 64–67, 103
  Śākyamuni. *See* Śākyamuni
  words of, 8, 17, 50–51
Buddha families, 9, 31–33, 72–76, 106–107
  Tathāgata or body family, 32, 72–76, 107
  Lotus or speech family, 32, 72–76, 107
  Vajra or wisdom-mind family, 32, 72–76, 107
  Jewel Family of Qualities, 32–33, 72–76, 103, 107
  Amoghasiddhi family of activity, 32, 107
Buddha wisdoms, 72, 85–86, 107–108
Buddhafields, 9, 70–72, 86, 89, 100, 103
Buddhaguhya, 11
Buddahood, 4, 20, 28–31, 45–46, 57–58, 65
Buddhas, 9, 63, 70–79, 103–106
  consorts of, 71–72, 79

cause. *See* Doctrine of Cause
channels, 34, 62
Chöd. *See* Tibetan Buddhism
compassion, 35, 65, 83, 87, 91, 106
completive phase. *See* meditation
consciousness, 29, 44, 73, 82, 94–98, 100, 108–109
contact, 29–30

ḍākinī (khadro), 23, 25, 65–66, 77–79, 104
damthsig-sempa (samaya-sattva), 31, 32
death, 30, 99–100, 103
desire, 25, 30, 37, 47, 55, 73, 79, 82, 83, 90, 91, 94–98, 101
Dhanasaṃskṛta, 13
Dharma, ix, 31, 64–65, 68–69, 71, 104
  of precept, 47, 50–54, 64
  of realization, 47, 50–54, 64
  refuge in, 64–67
  of result, 64
  spiritual, 1
  wheel of, 4, 47, 75, 105
  worldly, 1
dharmadhātu, 33, 40, 43, 46, 66, 72, 75, 85
dharmakāya. *See* kāyas

Index

Printed in the United States
by Baker & Taylor Publisher Services